CASE STUDIES IN
CULTURAL ANTHROPOLOGY

GENERAL EDITORS
George and Louise Spindler
STANFORD UNIVERSITY

———————

HANO
A Tewa Indian Community in Arizona

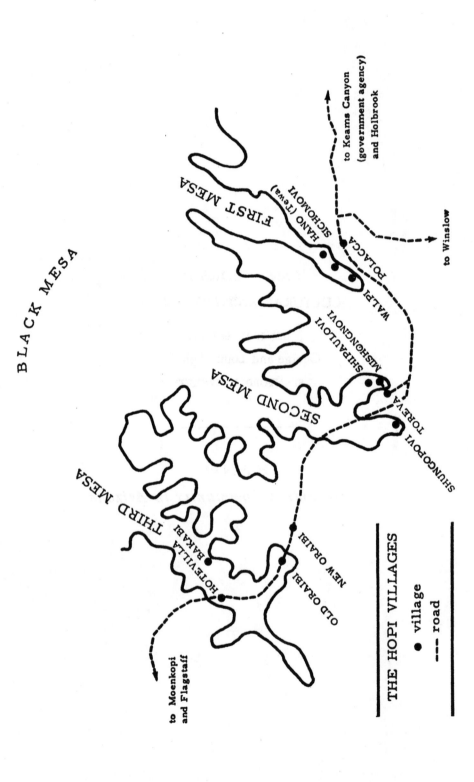

BLACK MESA

FIRST MESA

HANO (Tewa)
SICHOMOVI
POLACCA
WALPI

to Kearns Canyon
(government agency)
and Holbrook

to Winslow

SHIPAULOVI
MISHONGNOVI

SECOND MESA

OLD ORAIBI
TOREVA
SHUNGOPOVI

THIRD MESA

HOTEVILLA
BAKABI
NEW ORAIBI
OLD ORAIBI

to Moenkopi
and Flagstaff

THE HOPI VILLAGES

• village
-- road

HANO

A TEWA INDIAN COMMUNITY IN ARIZONA

Edward P. Dozier

CENGAGE
Learning™

Australia • Brazil • Japan • Korea • Mexico • Singapore • Spain • United Kingdom • United States

Hano: A Tewa Indian Community in Arizona

Edward P. Dozier

Executive Editor:
 Maureen Staudt
 Michael Stranz

Senoir Project Development Manager:
 Linda de Stefano

Marketing Specialist:
 Sara Mercurio
 Lindsay Shapiro

Production/Manufacturing Manager:
 Donna M. Brown

PreMedia Supervisor:
 Joel Brennecke

Rights & Permissions Specialist:

 Kalina Hintz
 Todd Osborne

Cover Image:
 Getty Images*

For product information and
technology assistance, contact us at **Cengage Learning Customer & Sales Support, 1-800-354-9706**

For permission to use material from this text or product, submit all requests online at **cengage.com/permissions** Further permissions questions can be emailed to **permissionrequest@cengage.com**

ISBN-13: 978-0-03-075653-5

ISBN-10: 0-03-075653-7

Cengage Learning
5191 Natorp Boulevard
Mason, Ohio 45040
USA

Cengage Learning is a leading provider of customized learning solutions with office locations around the globe, including Singapore, the United Kingdom, Australia, Mexico, Brazil, and Japan. Locate your local office at: **international.cengage.com/region**

Cengage Learning products are represented in Canada by Nelson Education, Ltd.

For your lifelong learning solutions, visit **www.cengage.com/custom**

Visit our corporate website at **www.cengage.com**

1 2 3 4 5 6 7 12 11 10 09 08

Foreword

About the Series

These case studies in cultural anthropology are designed to bring to students, in beginning and intermediate courses in the social sciences, insights into the richness and complexity of human life as it is lived in different ways and in different places. They are written by men and women who have lived in the societies they write about and who are professionally trained as observers and interpreters of human behavior. The authors are also teachers, and in writing their books they have kept the students who will read them foremost in their minds. It is our belief that when an understanding of ways of life very different from one's own is gained, abstractions and generalizations about social structure, cultural values, subsistence techniques, and the other universal categories of human social behavior become meaningful.

About the Author

Edward Dozier was born in the Tewa pueblo of Santa Clara. His mother, a full-blooded Tewa, was a student of his father, an American school teacher in the pueblo, when they married. Dr. Dozier's early life and schooling were in the pueblo.

The author became interested in anthropology quite early, and took both his B.A. and M.A. in anthropology at the University of New Mexico. He then attended the University of California at Los Angeles, where he obtained his Ph.D. degree in 1952. Since then he has taught at the University of Oregon and Northwestern University, and since 1960 has been a professor of anthropology at the University of Arizona, Tucson. In 1958–1959 he was a Fellow at the Center for Advanced Studies in the Behavioral Sciences at Stanford, California. He has done fieldwork in southwestern United States and among the Kalinga people of northern Luzon, Philippines. He has published *The Hopi-Tewa of Arizona, The Kalinga of Northern Luzon,* and numerous articles on anthropology in scholarly journals.

About the Book

This case study is unusual. It was written by a man who knows Hano, the Tewa Indian community of which he writes, in a somewhat different way than most anthropologists know pueblo communities. He is accepted as a friend, as an insider, and speaks the language fluently. He never violates this friendship and acceptance in what he writes about the Tewa, and yet the reader achieves a feeling of directness and intimacy that is often lacking in descriptions of pueblo life. This is also an unusual case study because the adaptation and assimilation of one way of life and one people to another non-Western society as well as to Western culture is described. This is indeed rare in anthropological literature.

The author gives us an understanding of the historical forces shaping so much of what we see today in the pueblo communities of which he writes. Besides giving us the history of the situation we encounter today in the pueblos, and an analysis of the adjustive interrelationships of Whites, Tewa Indians, and Hopi Indians, the author gives us a succinct and directly comprehensible description of the network of social relationships in the pueblo. His analysis is particularly notable for the clarity with which the behaviors and expectations connected with kinship terminology and group membership are described.

Dr. Dozier includes discussion of the religious and ritual associations and activities, and of the way in which people earn their living and share the products of their labors. He ends the case study with an overview of Tewa-Hopi interrelationships.

This case study will help fill a serious gap in the literature available to students on the pueblo communities of our own Southwest and adds significantly to our professional knowledge of one relatively unknown community.

GEORGE AND LOUISE SPINDLER
General Editors

Stanford, California
November 1965

Contents

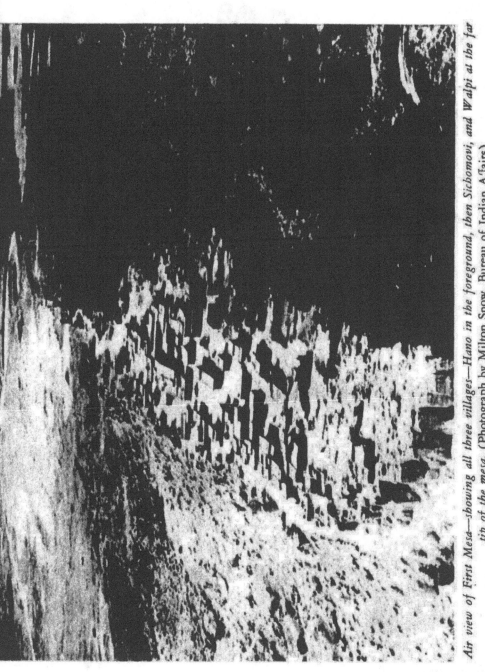

Air view of First Mesa—showing all three villages—Hano in the foreground, then Sichomovi, and Walpi at the far tip of the mesa. (Photograph by Milton Snow, Bureau of Indian Affairs)

Niman Kachina Dance. (Courtesy of Smithsonian Office of Anthropology, Bureau of American Ethnology Collection)

Left: Hano Tewa woman in ceremonial dress standing in front of Kiva. Right: Buffalo Dance at Santa Clara Pueblo, Rio Grande Tewa. (Courtesy of the Arizona State Museum)

Introduction

THE HOPI AND TEWA INDIANS living in the *mesa* country of Arizona are of two different cultural and linguistic traditions and have lived together for more than 250 years in close contact with one another, yet only in recent years have barriers fallen and the two groups begun to live harmoniously together.

The ancestors of the Hopi have been residents of the mesa-top villages for many centuries, but the Tewa are newcomers; they are the descendants of refugees from New Mexico who fled from Spanish oppression in the seventeenth century. The coming of the Spaniards was a major catastrophe to the peaceful Pueblo Indians residing along the Rio Grande and its tributaries in New Mexico. White man's diseases and the fanatical pogroms of the Spaniards to Christianize and "civilize" the Indians took a large toll of Pueblo lives. Many of these Indians fled their villages and joined the nomadic Apachean tribes, while others sought refuge amoung the sedentary Hopi.

First Mesa, the easternmost escarpment of the Hopi mesas, contains three villages: one of them is the Tewa community of Hano; the other two villages are Hopi. Further west on similar mesa-tops are other Hopi villages; only First Mesa, however, harbors a community different in speech and customs from the others.

The traditions of the Hopi and the Tewa indicate that the community of Hano remained in a minority status for a long time. Tewa inhabitants were denied full participation in Hopi ceremonies, and only the poorer plots of land were made available for them to farm. Hano, in return, clung tenaciously to its own cultural forms and carefully prevented the diffusion of its language and customs to its neighbors. In comparatively recent years this mutual pattern of resistance has broken down. The change appears to coincide with accelerated American activities, such as the establishment of the government agency and schools, the dissemination of stock-raising information, trading-post activities, the employment of Indians for wage work, and the influx of tourists.

The introduction of new activities alone has not produced the changes discussed in this report. The crucial factor appears to be a reorientation of the value system on First Mesa—a reorientation more compatible with Tewa values. There is abundant evidence that the Tewa demonstrated very early in the American period a willingness to cooperate with Americans and to participate in American activities. The personality of the Tewa proved congenial to Americans, and the Indians adjusted remarkably well to the changing situation brought about by American contact. The success of the Tewa in American activities seems to have resulted in reduced tensions and in emulation of the Tewa by their Hopi neighbors. This, in turn, paved the way for greater interdependence and cooperation among the three villages on First Mesa. As a consequence, the minority status of the Tewa began to dissolve, and the present trend toward an integrated First Mesa society commenced.

This report is based on field studies carried out on the Hopi reservation (which includes the Hano Tewa) over a number of years. I have also drawn from previous studies among the Tewa and Hopi, particularly those of Fred Eggan, Mischa Titiev, and Barbara Aitken. For the support of my fieldwork, I am indebted to the Social Science Research Council, the Wenner-Gren Foundation, and to an Opportunity Fellowship from the John Hay Whitney Foundation. This report also owes much to many Hopi and Tewa friends who gave generously of their time to give me deeper insight and understanding of Pueblo culture.

Rio Grande Homeland

A T THE TIME the first Spanish expedition entered the Rio Grande Pueblo country in 1540 the Tewa represented one of the largest language groups in the Southwest. The first census report of the Pueblos contained in the Memorial of Alonzo de Benavides 1634 (Hodge, Hammond, and Rey 1945) reported the population of the Tewa at 10,000 The Pueblo villages of the Tanoan linguistic group, of which the Tewa were a member (along with the Tiwa, Towa, and Piro), extended southward from Taos to near the present site of El Paso. They formed a barrier to the Plains Indians' encroachment from the east, and served as a buffer zone to the Keresan Pueblo communities farther west. The Tewa, divided into a northern and southern group, lived in the vicinity of Santa Fe. The Northern Tewa resided just north of the capital in what is now the Espanola Valley. Some of these villages have survived to the present time, and the pueblos of Tesuque, Nambe, San Ildefonso, Santa Clara, and San Juan carry many of the traditional Tewa cultural and social characteristics. Southward, including Santa Fe itself, were the pueblos of the Southern Tewa, designated in the early Spanish accounts as *Thano* or *Tano*. Historical and ethnological data indicate that there was little difference linguistically and culturally between the two Tewa groups. The early Spanish authorities separated the groups administratively, however, and apparently the southern branch gave the Spaniards the most trouble. After the Pueblo Indian revolt of 1680–1692, these Indians were dispersed among some of the more peaceful pueblos in order to quell their rebellious nature. For a brief period some of the Southern Tewa were resettled near the present site of Chimayo in the Northern Tewa country. Troubles with the Spaniards persisted, however, and in 1696 this group, the ancestors of the present Hano Tewa, fled to the Hopi country to escape Spanish oppression.

The kind of relations that existed between the Rio Grande Pueblos and the Spaniards during the early periods of contact is important in understanding the cultural conservatism of these Pueblos today. It is, therefore, germane to review these relations in greater detail.

Exploring Expeditions

The expedition of Francisco Vasquez de Coronado in 1540 brought the first white men seen by the Rio Grande Pueblo Indians. Coronado's party was a spectacular group of several hundred mailed and armed horsemen accompanied by Mexican Indian servants. The party crossed and recrossed the Tewa country several times during the two years they remained in the Pueblo country. From the beginning the Spaniards made themselves feared and distrusted. The expedition made incessant demands for food and other supplies, and in Coronado's headquarters at Tiguex (a Tiwa village), a lieutenant of Coronado executed several hundred Indians for a minor rebellion. The news of Spanish cruelty spread rapidly throughout the pueblos, and the seed of resentment and hatred for the white man had been sown.

The next expedition into the Pueblo country forty years later was a small one. The party was under the command of Francisco Sanchez Chamuscado, and included besides Chamuscado, a Franciscan priest (Father Augustin Rodriguez), two Franciscan brothers, and twelve soldiers. The party visited the Tewa pueblos, and upon its departure, left the friars among the pueblos, apparently in Tiwa pueblos.

A third expedition led by Antonio de Espejo was sent out in 1582 to find out the fate of the friars left by the Chamuscado expedition. The party included one Franciscan priest and fourteen soldiers. No evidence of the missionaries was found; obviously the friars had been put to death, but the Indians would not implicate anyone. Espejo explored the regions already visited by Coronado; he found nothing new, but he has left us probably the best detailed description of early Pueblo village life. It is interesting that with a few minor additions and deletions Espejo's account could serve as a description of Tewa pueblo life at the beginning of the present century, more than three hundred years later. The last sixty to seventy years has, of course, brought about tremendous material changes, but changes in the socio-cultural domain have been comparatively slight. The following excerpts from Espejo's report might be compared with a contemporary description of the villages and life-way of the Pueblos in order to comprehend Pueblo conservatism:

> As we were going through this province [the Piro country], from each pueblo the people came out to receive us, taking us to their pueblos and giving us a great quantity of turkeys, maize, beans, tortillas, and other kinds of bread. . . . They grind on very large stones. Five or six women together grind raw corn . . . and from this flour they make many different kinds of bread. They have houses of two, three, and four stories, with many rooms in each house . . . in each plaza of the towns they have two *estufas* [kivas], which are houses built underground, very well sheltered and closed, with seats of stone against the walls to sit on. Likewise, they have at the door of each *estufa* a ladder on which to descend, and a great quantity of community wood, so that strangers may gather there.
> In this province some of the natives wear cotton, cow hides [buffalo],

and dressed deerskin. . . . The women wear cotton skirts, many of them being embroidered with colored thread, and on top a *manta* like those worn by the Mexican Indians, tied around the waist with a cloth like an embroidered towel with a tassel . . . and all, men as well as women, dress their feet in shoes and boots, the soles being of cowhide and the uppers of dressed deerskin. The women wear their hair carefully combed and nicely kept in place by the moulds that they wear on their heads, one on each side, on which the hair is arranged very neatly, though they wear no headdress. In each pueblo they have their caciques. . . . These caciques have under them . . . *tequitatos,* who are like alguaciles [policemen], and who execute in the pueblo the cacique's orders. . . . And when the Spaniards ask the caciques of the pueblos for anything, they call the *tequitatos,* who cry it through the pueblo in a loud voice . . ..

. . . In each one of these pueblos they have a house to which they carry food for the devil, and they have small stone idols which they worship. Just as the Spaniards have crosses along the roads, they have between the pueblos, in the middle of the road, small caves or grottoes, like shrines, built of stones, where they place painted sticks and feathers, saying that the devil goes there to rest and speak with them.

They have fields of maize, beans, gourds, and *piciete* [tobacco] in large quantities. . . . Some of the fields are under irrigation, possessing very good diverting ditches, while others are dependent upon the weather. Each one has in his field a canopy with four stakes . . . where he takes his siesta, for ordinarily they are in their fields from morning until night. . . . Their arms consist of bows and arrows, *macanas* and *chimales;* the arrows have fire-hardened shafts, the heads being pointed flint, with which they easily pass through a coat of mail. The *chimales* are made of cowhide, like leather shields; and the *macanas* consist of rods half a vara long, with very thick heads. With them they defend themselves within their houses. It was not learned that they were at war with any other province. . . . (Bolton 1916:177–179)

Colonization

For more than a decade after Espejo's return to Mexico, he, as well as others, attempted to secure royal permission to colonize the Pueblo country. The contract for colonization was eventually awarded to Don Juan de Oñate in 1595. Oñate spent three years recruiting colonists and organizing an expeditionary force. The colonizing party consisting of several hundred Spaniards and Mexican Indians finally departed from southern Chihuahua in January 15, 1598, and entered the Pueblo country late that same year. Oñate established his headquarters near the Tewa Pueblo of San Juan, and by the end of the century had obtained the submission of all the major Pueblo groups. The seat of the provincial government was moved in 1610 to Santa Fe, the site of a former Southern Tewa village. From this headquarters the Christianizing and "civilizing" program was carried forth rapidly and energetically. Father Alonzo de Benavides, who came to implement the missionary program early in the century, reported in his *Memorial* of 1630 that 60,000 Pueblo Indians had been converted and ninety chapels built in as many villages.

From 1620 to the end of the century there were three main areas of Spanish colonization in the Pueblo country: (1) Santa Fe, (2) La Canada, near present Santa Cruz in the Tewa Basin, and (3) the southern district from Santo Domingo south to approximately the position of modern Socorro. In addition to these settlements, the more populous Pueblo villages had resident priests and sometimes a small guard of soldiers. The construction of ninety chapels by 1630 reported in Benavides' *Memorial* is probably correct, but only a few of these had resident missionaries. Most of the chapels were *visitas* to which a priest resident in another pueblo journeyed once a month to conduct Mass and other church services. All of the Pueblo villages, regardless of whether they had a resident missionary or not, however, became involved in the concerns and activities of the newcomers. Both civil authorities and missionaries abused the Indians either by exacting tribute or labor from them. Indeed, the competition for the services of the Indians resulted in a continuous conflict between civil and missionary authorities. This was a factor which contributed to the demoralization and disorganization of the New Mexico colony, and in part, at least, paved the way for the Pueblo Revolt of 1680.

Missionary Activities

In the initial period of colonization the missionaries were engaged in enormous construction programs. The mission buildings were large walled compounds within or just outside the Pueblo villages. They were constructed entirely by Indian labor under supervision of the friars. They were structures of adobe, or, in the case of the Eastern Tiwa and Piro Pueblos, of sandstone slabs set in adobe mud. Beams, doors, and window frames were of timber cut on steep mountain sides and brought a distance of twenty-five to thirty miles to mission sites by the Indians.

Within the mission compound lived one or two missionaries and a number of Indian workers and servants. Although the missions were supposed to be training centers for Indians, they served primarily as a place where the friars could live in comfort. Indians were employed at leatherwork, weaving, blacksmithing, and as cooks and servants. The mission also had grazing lands outside the compound where they kept sheep and cattle under the care of Indian herdsmen. Gardens and orchards were also a regular feature of the mission compound.

The religious responsibilities of the missionaries consisted of saying Mass, conducting burial services, performing baptisms and marriages, and conducting vesper services. A few Indians were taught prayers and made responsible for making the villagers attend church services.

The following description of church services are excerpted from a statement by the resident priest of Jemez Pueblo. Although the statement is contained in a report of conditions in the missions of New Mexico after the Pueblo Revolt of 1680, the description is probably valid for the period before the revolt as well:

The bell is rung at sunrise. The married men enter, each one with his wife, and they kneel together in a row on each side of the nave of the church. Each couple has its own place designated in accordance with the census list. When there are many, the married couples make two rows on each side, the two men in the middle and the women on the sides. This may seem a superficial matter, but it is not, for experience has taught me [the resident priest] that when these women are together they spend all the time dedicated to prayer and Mass in gossip, showing one another their glass beads, ribbons, medals, etc., telling who gave them or how they obtained them, and other mischief. Therefore the religious who has charge of the administration must have a care in this regard. After all, it is a house of prayer, not of chitchat. . . .

The petty governor and his lieutenant [Indians] have their places at the door so that the people may not leave during the hour of prayer and Mass.

When all are in their places, the fiscal mayor [an Indian] notifies the father, who comes down with his census lists and takes attendance to see whether everyone is there, whether they are in their proper places, and whether their hair is unbound. If anyone is missing, the petty governor goes to fetch him. If he is not in the pueblo, it is indicated by the thong [i.e., he is whipped] and he is punished on the following Sunday or holy day of obligation. If the truant is a woman, her husband is sent to fetch her. . . .

After Mass is over, if the minister thinks that some have left, he summons them in accordance with the list and punishes anyone who does such a thing. He severely reprimands the petty governor who permits it. . . .

The lists of married men and widowers are so arranged that if anyone is guilty of absence, this is indicated by the thong. . . . (Adams and Chavez 1956:308–15)

In addition to forcing attendance at Mass and other church services, the missionaries concentrated on the eradication of Pueblo customs and beliefs. Kivas were raided periodically and masks and prayer sticks burned. Pueblo religious leaders were whipped and hanged as witches if their activities became known to church and civil authorities. In the process the missionaries incurred the resentment of all the Indians, who, instead of giving up their beliefs and customs, went "underground" but lost none of their fervor for the native religion.

Secular Authorities

The supreme authority in the Spanish province of New Mexico was the governor and captain-general. He was appointed by the viceroy in Mexico City. The governors were supposed to promote the general welfare of the province: they were charged with the administration of justice, responsible for the protection of the settlers and Pueblos from outside enemies, and required to support the missionary program. Actually, however, the governors rarely complied with these duties. Almost all the governors during the seventeenth century engaged in various types of economic ventures for their own profit. In these ventures the labor and products of the Indian were used. Indians were made to spend long hours weaving cloth and blankets in workshops set up for the purpose in the pueblos and in Santa Fe. Other Indians were made to collect large quantities of piñon nuts, which brought a handsome price in Mexico. Still other Indians were employed to build wagons and carts for special caravans to Mexico. In the caravan trains Pueblo Indians were pressed into service as servants and muleteers.

The soldier-citizens, or *encomenderos*, were usually family heads whose responsibilities entailed the protection of the province from internal revolt and from attack by nomadic Indians. In fact, however, they were but instruments of the governors and served their interests more than the responsibilities they were supposed to fulfill. They received no pay, but the *encomiendas* which they received were far more profitable than salaries. The governor allocated the encomiendas to each soldier and determined the revenues to be derived from them. An encomienda in New Mexico entitled a soldier-citizen to the services of a number of Indians. Some of these Indians were household servants, but the main service they performed was the maintenance of farms and livestock for the benefit of the encomenderos.

In addition to the governor and encomenderos, the Spanish civil government system of the province included a secretary of government and war, a lieutenant governor, and *alcaldes mayores*. All were appointed by the governor and held office at his pleasure. The secretary was the governor's adviser and constant companion; he was in charge of all documents and papers issued in the governor's name. The lieutenant governors performed services and activities which the governor could not perform, represented the governor in his absence, and during the latter part of the century assumed control over the southern district. The *alcaldes mayores* administered subdivisions of the province. During the seventeenth century there were six or eight such units in New Mexico. These people dealt directly with the settlers and the Indians. They were perhaps without exception instruments of the governor and carried out his explicit orders. They and the soldier-citizens kept the recruitment of Indians for labor and the flow of tribute going. None of the officials below the governor received direct pay, but they all profited from the collection of tribute and from the labor of the Indians.

As the missionaries and colonial officials began to see the system of exploitation bearing fruit, they made more and more demands on the Indians. The Pueblos, by nature peaceful and unaggressive, were slow to react to the injustices and abuses to which they were subjected. Yet no people, no matter how passive or submissive, can remain completely unmoved when confronted by such oppression. The relations between the colonists and the Pueblos were, by the middle of the seventeenth century, at the danger point of eruption. The case of the Pueblos is admirably presented by Scholes:

> By 1650 the Indians were fully aware of the meaning and implications of Spanish supremacy and the mission system. Spanish supremacy had brought a heavy burden of labor and tribute and encroachment on the lands of the Pueblos. The mission system added to the burden of labor, but the most important phase of the program of Christianization was its effect on the old folk customs.
>
> The friars sought not only to teach a new faith, but they zealously tried also to put an end to the practice of native religious ceremonial, to destroy the influence of the traditional leaders of the Indians, and to impose rigid

monogamy on a people whose code of marital and sexual relationship was fairly flexible and elastic. In order to maintain mission discipline the friars often resorted to the imposition of physical punishment for such offenses as failure to attend religious services, sexual immorality, and participation in the native ceremonial dances.

But drastic disciplinary measures . . . could not force full allegiance to the new order. The efforts of the clergy to abolish the old ceremonial forms and to set up new standards of conduct merely caused greater resentment on the part of the Indians. . . . The Pueblos were not unwilling to accept externals of the new faith, but they found it difficult to understand the deeper spiritual values of Christianity. Pueblo religion served definite material and social ends, viz., the propitiation of those supernatural forces which they believed controlled their daily existence. They expected the same results from the Christian faith. But they soon realized that the new ways were no more successful in obtaining a good harvest than the old, and they realized too that the efforts to abolish their traditional ceremonials and destroy the influence of the old native leaders whose functions were both social and religious, raised serious problems concerning the entire fund of Pueblo civilization. Bewilderment soon turned into resentment, and resentment into a resurgence of loyalty to the traditional norms of folk-culture. The burden of labor and tribute might have been tolerated if offset by recognized advantages, but if the new was no more efficient in guaranteeing a harvest or success in the hunt, what had been gained by accepting Spanish overlordship? (Scholes 1942:11, 15-16)

A number of minor and local revolts were repressed, but in 1680 the Pueblos successfully carried out a general revolt under the leadership of the San Juan Tewa Indian, Popé. Popé had been one of forty-seven Pueblo religious leaders given a public whipping in Santa Fe by Spanish authorities in 1675. Smarting under the punishment, Popé planned a general revolt from his headquarters which he established in Taos Pueblo. The news of the uprising leaked out before the day planned for its execution, and the revolt had to be put into effect prematurely. The rebellion lasted for only about three weeks, but for battles fought with the crude firearms of the Spanish settlers and the bows and arrows of the Indians, it was a ferocious and bloody one. At the end of the revolt, 21 missionaries and 375 colonists were dead, while another 2000 settlers had been driven out of the Pueblo country. The Tewa and the Northern Tiwa Pueblos were the most active in the revolt and suffered the most casualties. In two skirmishes alone, 300 Southern Tewa besieging Santa Fe were killed and 47 others captured and executed. The Piro Pueblos and the Pueblo of Isleta did not take part in the revolt, but all the other Pueblos aided the general revolt by killing their resident missionaries and other colonists living in or near these pueblos. The Apaches apparently did not participate actively, but the Spaniards were led to believe they were in the revolt pact and therefore succumbed more readily. Mission establishments were destroyed everywhere, and their furnishings and records burned. Much of the destruction occurred after the colonists had quit the Pueblo country. Statements issued by Indians captured in an abortive reconquest attempt in 1681–1682 by Governor Antonio de Otermin uniformly attested that the leaders of the rebellion wanted to wipe out every vestige of

Catholic religion. The declaration of two brothers from the pueblo of San Felipe is typical of the statements recorded by Otermin:

> Asked what happened after the said rebellion [the two brothers] said they saw that the said Indian, Popé, came down to the pueblo of San Felipe accompanied by many captains from the pueblos and by other Indians and ordered the churches burned and the holy images broken up and burned. They took possession of everything in the sacristy pertaining to divine worship, and said that they were weary of putting in order, sweeping, heating, and adorning the church; and that they proclaimed both in the said pueblo and in the others that he who should utter the name of Jesus would be killed immediately; and that they [the Indians] were not to pray or to live with the wives whom they had taken in holy matrimony, all under the said penalty of death; and that thereupon they could live contentedly, happy in their freedom, living according to their ancient custom. . . .
>
> They declared further that by order of the said Popé and of Alonso Catiti, governor and head of the Queres nation, they were commanded to place in the pueblo and its environs piles of stones on which they could offer ground corn and other cereals and tobacco, they saying that the stones were their God, and that they were to observe this, even to the children, giving them to understand that thereby they would have everything they might desire. They say that they have passed over many other things that they do not recall, but they saw that as soon as the señor governor and the rest of the Spaniards had left, the Indians erected many estufas in the pueblos and danced the dances of the cazina and of losse [masked Kachina and the clown or Koshare dances], which are dances instituted by the devil. . . . (Hackett and Shelby 1942:251)

Each pueblo community is an independent social and political entity; even those villages of the same language group lack an over-all political organization. Until the Pueblos were confronted by the superior arms and tactical skills of the Spaniards their pattern of resistance had been in the form of small and brief offensive and defensive encounters with other Indian enemies no better organized or equipped than they were. It was the recognition of a common grievance—the abuses and injustices suffered by the oppressive acts of Spanish religious and civil authorities—which brought the Pueblos together temporarily. As soon as the Spaniards were out of the area, the temporary unity dissolved. Controversy and dissension broke loose, and the Pueblos began to bicker among themselves, and refuse to listen to their temporary leaders. To make matters worse, the Apaches, realizing that Spanish intervention had been removed, stepped up their raids on the marginal pueblo villages. To escape the ravages of the Apaches and apprehensive of a returning Spanish punitive or reconquest expedition, the Pueblo Indians retreated into more defensible areas in the mountains and mesas. The Southern Tewa abandoned their pueblos and part of them moved into Santa Fe, while the rest established settlements near the present site of Santa Cruz among their northern linguistic relatives.

Governor Otermin attempted an unsuccessful reconquest in the winter of 1681–1682, and there were two other unsuccessful forays by Governor Pedro Reneros de Posada in 1688 and Governor Cruzate in 1689. It was Don Diego de Vargas under a well-equipped army who finally reestablished Spanish control of the Pueblos in 1693. The Tiwa and Keresan Pueblos submitted without a struggle, and they were persuaded by De Vargas to return to their pueblos peaceably. The Southern Tewa group entrenched in Santa Fe at first threatened to fight, but De Vargas took the city without firing a shot. Indians were given to soldiers and colonists as slaves, while others were settled among the Northern Tewa villages. Those Southern Tewa who had established settlements near Santa Cruz refused to surrender, however. These Tewa carried on a hit and run warfare with De Vargas from the top of Black Mesa near San Ildefonso. They withstood the attacks of Spanish soldiers for nine months, but were finally compelled to sue for peace and return to their villages.

De Vargas quickly resettled the areas formerly occupied by Spanish and Mexican colonists and founded a new villa (Santa Cruz) in the heart of the Northern Tewa country. The new settlement took in the pueblos and lands occupied by the Southern Tewa who were resettled in a single village in the vicinity of what is now Chimayo. By repossessing the lands of the Pueblos and by reintroducing some of the abuses of the prerevolt period, De Vargas again brought general discontentment among the Pueblos. Early in June of 1696, the Tewa (including the resettled Southern Tewa) together with the Indians of Taos, Picuris, Santa Domingo, and Cochiti rose in revolt. Twenty-one Spaniards and six priests were killed. De Vargas quickly put an end to the uprising, but before he could reach the Tewa area, the entire population of the resettled Southern Tewa community had fled to the Hopi country.

By the end of the century the Pueblo area had been drastically reduced. All the Piro pueblos were uninhabited as were also the Tiwa villages east of the mountains and along the Rio Grande south of Isleta pueblo. Some of these Indians had joined the Spaniards retreating south in 1680 and founded communities below El Paso, while others migrated to the Navaho and Hopi country. The aftermath of the revolt and reconquest reduced the Pueblo communities to essentially the sites they occupy today.

The flight of the remnant Southern Tewa group to the Hopi country completes the history of this formerly significant Pueblo population in the Rio Grande area. We will resume their history in their new home shortly, but at present it is important to consider the effects of almost one hundred years of Spanish rule.

Effects of Spanish Rule

Contact with Spaniards brought about obvious changes among the pueblos. A Catholic chapel became a prominent feature of the community, and in the larger villages, a mission compound and workshops as well. These additions intended by Spanish authorities to be central features of the villages rarely became such. In all but a few pueblos the center of the community was moved away from the missionary buildings and the village courtyard, where the ceremonial chamber or chambers (the kivas) were rebuilt, continued to be the hub of social and ceremonial life.

Early in the seventeenth century Spanish authorities imposed a civil government system on the Pueblos. As an aid to the missionary program and civil administration, the pueblos were required to appoint a set of officers to meet with the Spaniards. Among the Pueblos, these officers were usually a governor, a lieutenant governor, an *alguacil*, or sheriff, a sacristan, *mayordomos*, and *fiscales*. The governor was to represent the village in all important dealings with Spanish authorities. The lieutenant governor was to serve as assistant to the governor and represent him when absent, and, in the event of the governor's death, succeed him. The sheriff was to maintain law and order within the pueblo; the sacristan was church assistant and aid to the priest; the fiscales were responsible for mission discipline, while the mayordomos were ditch superintendents. But the civil government system did not displace the native socio-political organization, and to this day the native socio-political system remains the *de facto* governmental and ceremonial organization. The Tewa migrant group apparently discarded the civil government system altogether upon reaching the Hopi country, for there is no vestige of such a system at Hano today.

The effect of Spanish indoctrination on the values and beliefs of the Pueblo Indians appears to be negligible. Undoubtedly the ancestors of the Southern Tewa in New Mexico went to Mass, confessed, received communion, attended vespers, and were baptized, married, and buried by friars for almost a century. All of these practices were abandoned at Hopi, and nothing remains to indicate that Christianity was ever a part of Hano society and culture.

The resistance to change and to adopt other than material items and surface behavioral patterns from any culture are thought by many students of Pueblo culture to be deeply rooted in the indigenous past of these people. It is not possible to demonstrate such a supposition, but the contact conditions were so oppressive that no people no matter how permissive to the acceptance of alien social and cultural items could have been expected to remain for long receptive to innovations brutally forced upon them while their own indigenous practices were being viciously suppressed. When we add to this the later coercive treatment meted out to the Pueblos by Anglo-Americans we need not seek further to explain Pueblo resistance patterns. The astute observations of John C. Bourke, an early American student of the Pueblos, is pertinent here:

> The eradication of ideas rooted in the traditions of centuries and entwined with all that a nation holds lovable and sacred is beyond the decree of a Council or the order of a military Commander. Unable to practice their ancient rites in public, the Pueblos cling to them all the more tenaciously because the double halo of danger and mystery now surrounded them. The Pueblos became hypocrites; they never became Catholics. Instances without number could possibly be adduced to those among them who sloughed off the exuviae of Paganism; or of others again who modified early teachings by ingrafting upon them the doctrines of the missionaries; but the great bulk of the population remained and today remain, Pagan and Anti-Christian. (Bloom 1936:262)

It is not surprising that the immigrant Tewa carried with them to the Hopi country the resistant patterns they had learned so well during a period of almost one hundred years of Spanish rule. We will chronicle the relations of these immigrants with their new neighbors in the next section.

2

At Hopi

THE HOPI PUEBLOS were also a part of Spain's northern province, but great distance, the lack of profitable natural resources, and the general inhospitality of the environment isolated the Hopi country from the provincial capital in Santa Fe. The major Spanish expeditions had all visited the Hopi villages, however. In 1540, a party of the Coronado expedition spent several days among the Hopi, and the Espejo expedition forty years later visited all the Hopi villages. Oñate, the colonizer of New Mexico, obtained the formal submission of the Hopi in 1598, and between 1629 and 1641 missions were established at Awatobi, Shongopovi, and Oraibi with chapels at Mishongnovi and Walpi. For a period of about fifty years the Hopi, therefore, experienced the coercive Spanish missionary program. During this period they submitted to the demands of labor and outwardly accepted Catholicism. When the Rio Grande Pueblos revolted in 1680, however, the Hopi killed their resident missionaries and destroyed the missions along with all furnishings. In 1692 realizing the futility of opposing a superior force, they submitted to De Vargas, the reconqueror of the northern province of New Spain.

The Pueblo rebellion and the abortive revolts of 1696 brought refugees from the Rio Grande. The Hopi harbored these refugees, undoubtedly in order to better resist the Spaniards and also to fight off the increasing raids of nomadic Indians. Indeed, the Tewa migration legend reports specifically that the Tewa were invited to First Mesa as mercenaries to drive off Ute Indian invaders.

The first mention of the Tewa at Hopi is made in Fray Jose Narvaez Valverde's account of the destruction of Awotovi. After the reconquest Awatovi, the most eastern of the Hopi villages, again accepted Spanish missionaries. When this news spread to the Hopi villages, the Hopi were incensed and the Tewa on First Mesa more than any of the others. Delegations from all the important villages met and decided to destroy Awatovi. Under the leadership of Espeleta, the Chief of Oraibi, warriors from all the villages, including those from Hano, fell upon Awatovi and in one night and one day of vicious fighting and destruction wreaked havoc on the village. Almost the entire population of the village said to number about 800 was massacred; only a few women and children were spared and later distributed among the other Hopi villages. Awatovi was completely destroyed and since that day has remained unoccupied.

The following is excerpted from Valverde's account. The Southern Tewa are here, as in the early Spanish reports, referred to as Thanos or Tanos:

> At this time, his people being infuriated because the Indians of the pueblo of Aguatubi [Awatovi] had been reduced to our holy faith and the obedience of our king, he [Espeleta, the chief of Oraibi] came with more than one hundred of his people to the said pueblo, entered it, killed all the braves, and carried off the women, leaving the pueblo to this day desolate and unpeopled. Learning of this outrage, Governor Don Pedro Rodriguez Cubero made ready some soldiers to punish it, and in the following year of 1701 went to the said province of Moqui [Spanish designation for the Hopi], taking with him the aforesaid religious, Fray Juan Caricochea and Fray Antonio Miranda. With his armed force he killed some Indians and captured others, but not being very well prepared to face the multitudes of the enemy, he withdrew and returned without being able to reduce them, especially as the Moquis had with them the Tanos Indians, who, after committing outrages had taken refuge among them and had risen at their command. (Narváez 1937:386)

Franciscan missionaries tried unsuccessfully to convert the Hopi during the first half of the eighteenth century. A number of Spanish governors also attempted to bring back the Rio Grande Pueblo Indians who had taken refuge among the Hopi. In August 1716 an army of Spaniards and Pueblo Indians under the command of Governor Felix Martinez made a futile attempt to bring back the Tewa. Martinez described his encounter with the Tewa as follows:

> . . . I explained to them [the Tewa] the sole purpose for which I had come with the army, this is, that they should offer submission to the Divine and human Majesty and bring back all of the Indians who had rebelled, some in the year '80 [1680] and others in '96 [1696]; that they should return to their own pueblos whence they fled. . . . (Bloom 1931: 204–205)

The Tewa refused to submit, however, and Martinez fired on their village killing eight Indians and wounding many others. The Spanish governor then proposed to the Hopi on First Mesa that he be allowed to ascend the Mesa and take the Tewa prisoners. According to Martinez the Hopi Cacique at Walpi "made a proclamation":

> . . . that they [the Walpi] were already friends with the Spaniards and did not desire the friendship of the said Thanos; that they will be severely punished for the harm they have done in making war . . . that many of their people had been killed and wounded through the fault of the said Thanos. . . . (Bloom 1931:218)

The Spaniards were assured that they could ascend the Mesa without being molested by the Hopi. Martinez apparently decided the venture would be too costly, however, and instead he ordered his men to destroy Tewa crops in the fields that were ready to be harvested and to kill all their livestock. "When all but a few very insignificant fields had been destroyed," Martinez felt that "the enemies of our Holy Faith" had been effectively punished and returned to Santa Fe.

Distance, the growing hostility of the nomadic tribes, and the dwindling resources of Spain all helped to keep the Hopi country isolated for another century. Toward the close of the eighteenth century Father Silvestre Velez Escalanta, seeking a route to California, spent a few days among the Hopi. The visit was apparently a friendly one. The following excerpt from Father Escalante's report mentions the Tewa on First Mesa and gives an account of their neighbors:

> . . . On the western point of the first [mesa] and on its most narrow eminence are situated three of the pueblos. The first is that of Janos (there they say Teguas) who use a tongue different from that of the Moqui. It is an ordinary pueblo with its little plaza in the middle and will include one hundred and ten families. The second to the east [west?] about a stone's throw. It has only fifteen families because of the new settlement which the Moqui are making at Gualpi. This is within gunshot of the second. It is larger than the two preceding ones and accommodates two hundred families. . . .
> This province is bounded on the east by the Navajos, on the west and northwest by the Cosninas [Havasupai], on the north by the Utes, on the southwest with others whom they call here Mescaleros. . . . The Moqui are very civilized, apply themselves to weaving and cultivating the land by means of which they raise abundant crops of maize, beans and chile. They also gather cotton although not much. They suffer from scarcity of wood and good water. . . . (Thomas 1932:150–52)

Mexico gained its independence from Spain in 1823, and the former northern province of Spain became a part of the new nation. During the brief Mexican interlude from 1823 to 1848 when New Mexico was annexed by the United States there were no reports of consequence about the Tewa and their Hopi neighbors. This was a difficult period for Mexico's northern possession. Spanish civil and church authorities had their hands full serving the Rio Grande Pueblos and a growing Hispanicized mestizo population. To make matters worse the vigorous Comanche Indians of the southern Plains had begun to raid the settlers and Pueblo Indians of New Mexico. The provincial government in Santa Fe was in no position to send missionaries to the Hopi country nor to provide military aid to these Indians who were likewise being besieged by Navaho and Ute raiders.

The deplorable condition of the Hopi Indians and the Rio Grande Pueblo refugees among them was highlighted in 1850 by a delegation which came to see James C. Calhoun, the First Agent of the Indians of the Territory of New Mexico. The purpose of the visit was to ascertain the "purposes and views of the government of the United States towards them" and to complain "bitterly of the depredations of the Navajos." It is interesting that the leader of the group "the Cacique of all the [Hopi] Pueblos" was from the Tewa village of Hano. (Official correspondence of James C. Calhoun, letter dated October 12, 1850).

The first eye-witness account of the Hopi and Tewa pueblos by an American is contained in a report by Dr. P. S. G. Tenbroeck, a surgeon in the United States Army, who visited the Hopi country in 1852:

> The inhabitants [of Hopi] all speak the same language except those of Harno [Hano], the most northern town of the three [on First Mesa; Hano, Sichomovi, Walpi], which has a different language and some customs peculiar to itself. It is, however, considered one of the towns of the confederation, and joins in all the feasts. It seems a very singular fact that, being within 150 yards of the middle town, Harno should have preserved for so long a period its own language and customs. The other Moquis say the inhabitants of this town have a great advantage over them, as they perfectly understand the common language, and none but the people of Harno understand their dialect. It is the smallest town of the three. (U.S. Department of the Interior 1894:171)

Navaho depredations finally came to an end when the Navaho were rounded up and removed to eastern New Mexico by Colonel Christopher ("Kit") Carson in 1863. The Navaho were returned to their homeland in 1868 and have since lived at peace with their Indian and white neighbors.

Contact between the Hopi and Anglo-Americans steadily increased after the pacification of the Navaho. Traders and Protestant missionaries arrived about 1870 and a mission school was established in 1875 at Keams Canyon twelve miles north of First Mesa. In 1869 a special agent for the Hopi Indians was appointed and in 1882 the Hopi Indian Reservation of 3863 square miles was set aside by executive order. A government school was opened at Keams Canyon in 1887. The First Mesa Hopi and the Tewa at Hano received the school enthusiastically, but most of the Hopi were indifferent; the Hopi community of Oraibi refused to send any children to the school.

In recent years the physical isolation of the Hopi country has almost completely dissolved. Automobile roads from Gallup, Holbrook, Winslow, and Flagstaff bring a constant stream of visitors. The colorful ceremonies of the Hopi attract large numbers of tourists; the Snake Dance ceremony alone draws a crowd of several thousand spectators annually.

A constitution was drawn up by the Hopi in 1936 with the aid of the United States government under the provisions of the Indian Reorganization Act. The Constitution was an attempt at self-government through the formation of a tribal government composed of representatives from each village. The innovation was completely unfamiliar to the Hopi, and the council has not worked out as anticipated. The Hopi villages have not functioned as a unit in the past and do not seem ready to do so at present. First Mesa has achieved a remarkable degree of social and political integration in recent years, but this is not true of the other Hopi village groups. The role of the Tewa in this integration is important and will be discussed in a subsequent section.

The externals of Hopi and Tewa society and culture have been affected profoundly by white American contact. Most of the material possessions come from the outside, and English as a secondary language is spoken by the majority of the Hopi and Tewa. Wage work and livestock have been added to horticultural activities and are now important in the economic structure. On the other hand, important aspects of the social and ceremonial organization and the religious concepts of the Hopi and Tewa remain unaffected.

The preceding has been a review of the historical events dealing with the Pueblos that has been gleaned from Spanish and American historical sources. It has not been possible to isolate the Tewa specifically in this review, for Southwestern historians tend to lump all Pueblo Indians together to present the interests and concerns primarily of the chroniclers. We hope, however, that the struggle of a people to survive physically as a group has emerged from the account. In the next few pages the Tewa's own version of their history is briefly reviewed. As is true with the traditions of most nonliterate peoples, the Tewa's account of their past is largely magical and fanciful. How much of the information they have passed down by word of mouth from one generation to another is fact and how much myth would be impossible to determine. Tewa "history" does give us insights, however, about their persistent desire to preserve cultural identity in a situation that seems favorable to rapid and complete assimilation.

Traditional History

According to a legend that the Tewa at Hano have kept alive from generation to generation, First Mesa Hopi chiefs had specifically invited the Tewa to come to the Hopi country. The reputation of the Tewa as relentless and fearless warriors had reached the Hopi and they wanted the Tewa to drive off their enemies. The invitation and rewards offered to the Tewa to persuade them to come to Hopi is contained in the following brief excerpt from the legend:

> Four times the Walpi Bear Clan Chief and Snake Clan Chief [Hopi clans on First Mesa] came to our village at *Tsawadeh*[1] [former home of the Southern Tewa in New Mexico]. They brought with them prayer sticks that represented the things that would be given to us if we would come and fight their enemies. There was one for the women that were promised to our men; there was one for the village site that we would occupy; there was one for the springs from which we would obtain our drinking water; there was one for the land on which we could raise our corn and other crops. . . . They drew for us on the sand the large stalks of corn that were raised on the land that would be ours. They extended both arms to indicate the size of the ears of corn that grew on this land. "All this will be yours if you will come and live among us as our protectors," they said. "In our land you will have plenty to eat and your storehouses will always be full."

According to the legend the Tewa accepted the invitation as a humane service to a Pueblo people, much like themselves, who were being besieged relentlessly by their enemies. It is interesting that the legend makes no mention of difficulties with the Spaniards as a reason for accepting the Hopi invitation. The

---

[1] See Orthographic Note on page 100.

Hano migration legend mythically recounts the journey from the Rio Grande to the Hopi country, and while references to the Spaniards and other Rio Grande Pueblo groups are made, there are no expressions of antagonistic feelings toward any of these people. Apparently the oppressive treatment suffered by the original migrants became less important and eventually forgotten by succeeding generations of the Tewa at Hano who had not actually experienced Spanish rule. Later generations found the injustices and ill-treatment directed at them by their Hopi hosts more important to record in their traditional history. The Tewa migration legend reports that upon the arrival of their ancestors at Hopi, they were treated as unwelcome intruders and none of the promises which had induced them to make the journey were forthcoming

> How pitifully ignorant must have been our ancestors to believe the Hopi! [regarding the rewards promised] Little did they know that they would be so miserably deceived. . . . Our grandmothers and grandfathers were not permitted to ascend the mesa [First Mesa] when they arrived at Hopi, but were forced to make camp below. When some of them petitioned Walpi women for food, they were told to cup their hands to receive a corn-meal gruel and boiling hot, it was poured into their hands. When the Tewa let the gruel slip to the ground and proceeded to nurse their burnt hands, the Hopi women laughed and berated them for being weak and soft.
> . . . When our ancestors had defeated the Utes and made life safe for the Hopi, they asked for the land, women, and food which had been promised to them. But the Hopi refused to give them these things. Then it was that our poor ancestors had to live like beasts, foraging on the wild plants and barely subsisting on the meager supply of food. Our ancestors lived miserably, beset by disease and starvation. The Hopi, well-fed and healthy, laughed and made fun of our ancestors.

The legend says that there were repeated attacks by the enemy for some time after their arrival in the Hopi country which were all successfully repelled by the Tewa. The reputation of the Tewa as fierce and courageous warriors spread among the nomadic tribes, however, and they stopped raiding the Hopi villages. Still the Hopi remained ill-tempered and their conduct was so ignoble and ungracious that the Tewa placed a "curse" on them:

> Our clan chiefs dug a pit between Hano and the Hopi villages [on First Mesa] and told the Hopi clan chiefs to spit into it. When they had all spat, our clan chiefs spat above the spittle of the Hopi. The pit was refilled, and then our clan chiefs declared:
> "Because you have behaved in a manner unbecoming to human beings, we have sealed knowledge of our language and our way of life from you. You and your descendants will never learn our language and our ceremonies, but we will learn yours. We will ridicule you in both your language and our own."

The particulars of the "curse" differ among Tewa story tellers, but the essential points are in all of them. Like all Pueblo traditions, those of the Tewa are couched in a mystical fanciful language; it is impossible to tell what is fact or fancy in the migration legend. No explanation, for example, is given, as to how the Hopi clan chiefs, more numerous than their Tewa counterparts, were made to spit into the pit. The implication is that Tewa magic was so powerful that the Hopi automatically followed the dictates of the Tewa clan chiefs. More difficult for practical-minded Western Europeans to understand is that the curse "worked." The Tewa were able "to sell" the curse to their neighbors and to have it work in their favor. The Hopi believe in the consequences of the curse as strongly as the Tewa. For both groups the prophecy has been fulfilled: the Hopi do not speak the Tewa language and they know little or nothing about the ceremonial life and other important customs of Tewa culture. How this may have been accomplished will be explored in the next section. Suffice to say, at present, supernatural sanctions exert a strong influence in prescribing and limiting behavior.

For the Tewa, the legend and the curse, which is perhaps the most fundamental feature of the legend, has been a kind of sacred and prophetic guide of their cultural tradition. The legend is related constantly in Hano homes; children grow up knowing it intimately, and among the stories and tales regularly recited in the kivas, the legend has a prominent place. The Hopi-Tewa delight in telling it to New Mexico Tewa visitors, thus belittling their neighbors. The legend is a kind of a model for proper behavior, as well, but perhaps its most important function has been the preservation of Tewa self-esteem. To a persecuted minority group, this function of the legend is essential to maintain group identity and pride. The survival and persistence of the Tewa cultural island in the midst of the generalized Hopi culture is undoubtedly reinforced by constant reference to it.

3

Hano—The Tewa Community

THE HOPI MESAS on which Hano and the other villages are situated are the southern spurs of Black Mesa, a high plateau which extends northward almost to the Utah border. The elevation of the villages is about 6000 feet above the sea, while the dry washes below are about 600 feet lower. The early American travelers who entered the Hopi country from the east designated the fingerlike projections as First, Second, and Third Mesa. On First Mesa are the villages of Hano, Sichomovi, and Walpi, and below the mesa is Polacca. Twelve miles beyond is Second Mesa with Mishongnovi, Shipaulovi, and Shongopovi. Another ten miles westward is Third Mesa with Old Oraibi at its tip and a recent community, New Oraibi, at its base. A mile or so beyond Oraibi, still on top of Third Mesa, is Hotevilla and a half mile northeastward, Bakabi. Forty miles farther west is Moenkopi, a colony founded about fifty years ago by members of the Third Mesa villages.

The Hopi country is an arid but picturesque land. Several miles north of the Hopi villages, Black Mesa supports a forest of piñon and juniper, but where the Hopi live, what trees might have grown have been used long ago for firewood. Only an occasional sage or rabbit brush struggles for existence. Curiously, a few twisted, dwarfed fruit trees (peaches, apricots, pears, and apples) dot the base of the mesas at places where moisture-bearing sands or seepage from springs provide enough water. These trees are grown from seeds or cuttings taken from trees originally introduced by the Spaniards. Most impressive about the land are the vistas—perhaps nowhere in America can one see so far—across sandy plains, isolated table outcrops and isolated buttes to distant outlines of blue mountains. In winter and spring the land is barren and windswept, but in late summer and fall it can be astonishingly beautiful. At this time clouds cast shadows near and far while occasional patches of sunlight enhance the rugged topography of the land. The villages themselves appear to be a part of the mesa rock outcroppings. Only one familiar with the location of the villages can detect them from below, so much are they of the same color and outline as the mesa itself.

However picturesque the Hopi country may be, it is an inhospitable environment for subsistence farmers. Except for a small stream which provides an irregular supply of irrigation water for the Hopi farmers of Moenkopi, none of the Hopi villages have access to permanently flowing streams. The plateau of Black Mesa acts as a reservoir, however, and at the base of the Hopi mesas are numerous springs which provide drinking water for the Hopi. In some springs the flow of water is abundant enough to permit the construction of small terraced gardens. These gardens merely add to the food supply; however, they are not sufficient to furnish food to feed even a small portion of a village. The Hopi subsist by dry farming in an extremely precarious environment. Annual precipitation is only about ten inches and this falls mainly in late summer, often too late to help mature crops. Maize, beans, and melons are planted near flat washes below the mesas where sands retain moisture and flash floods may hopefully irrigate the plants without uprooting them. In good years a fairly abundant harvest is taken in and stored to tide the Hopi over the lean years. But good years are the exception rather than the rule. Often there is so little rain that plants wither and die; at other times the rain falls in such torrents that the plants are washed away. The technology of the Hopi is so simple that little can be done in a practical way to solve the subsistence problem. It is no wonder that they have turned to magic to try to offset the hazards of wresting a living from an inhospitable environment. The Hopi have an elaborate ceremonial organization and engage in complex ritualistic activities that contrast sharply with the more simple and practically oriented socio-ceremonial organization of the Tewa. These differences are perhaps most marked between the two societies, but there are other important contrasts that will become evident in this and subsequent sections.

On First Mesa Hano houses merge in with those of the middle village, Sichomovi. Walpi, the third village, is located at the very tip of the mesa and is separated from Sichomovi by a narrow neck, barely fifteen feet in width. Despite the fact that Hano is contiguous with Sichomovi, the Tewa are keenly aware of the boundary that separates the two villages. At the foot of First Mesa and running roughly parallel to the villages on top is a recently settled community of both Hopi and Tewa called Polacca. Polacca was named after a Tewa man who was one of the first to settle below the mesa. An interpreter and friend of the whites, he was persuaded by Christian missionaries to build his home away from his native village. Most of today's inhabitants at Polacca, however, are not Christians; many of them are traditionalists and own houses on top of the mesa as well. The population of Polacca is constantly shifting; its inhabitants alternate freely in residence between houses at Hano and Polacca. Much of this alternation is dictated by ceremonial activities; when ceremonies are in progress, Hopi and Tewa Indians return to residences on top of the mesa. Polacca residents identify village allegiance with respect to the communities on top; hence, an individual will say he is from Walpi, or Sichomovi, or Hano, though he may be living at Polacca.

Walpi is considered the ceremonial center of First Mesa by all three villages. In Hopi thinking, time of arrival and length of residence is considered the important measure of village status and prestige. Walpi reports long residence on First Mesa and considers itself preeminent over both Hano and Sichomovi because its settlers arrived earlier. Sichomovi adheres strictly to Walpi's socioceremonial calendar and is considered simply a colony of that village. Hano enjoys a certain amount of social and ceremonial independence, concessions gained over a long period of quarreling, threats, and negotiations with Walpi.

In listing the population figures for First Mesa, Polacca will be excluded since its inhabitants align themselves with one of the three villages on top of the mesa. The approximate populations for each of the three villages on First Mesa are as follows: Hano 500, Sichomovi 400, Walpi 600. About one-third of the inhabitants of First Mesa are Tewa, but compared to the total Hopi population of about 5000, the Tewa comprise only one-tenth of the whole. We have no figures for the number of Tewa who came to the Hopi country in 1696, but in 1775 Father Escalante (see Chapter 2) reported the population of Hano as 110 families. If we project the average size family of present-day Hano, five to an elementary family, the population of Hano at the time of Escalante's visit would be nearly the same as the present population. Hopi and Tewa populations today represent an increase from 2338 in 1904 when smallpox epidemics had drastically reduced the population. On this date the population of the Tewa at Hano was listed at only 160. With the control of smallpox and the introduction of modern health measures, Hopi and Tewa populations rapidly increased to the present figure of over 5000. Hopi and Tewa population increases coincide with those of the Pueblos generally and the Navaho as well. Rates of population gain among these Indians are far above the national average over the past half century.

In outward appearances Hano looks like a typical Hopi village. Its houses, like those in which the Hopi live, are constructed of stone; they are flat-roofed; and the walls on the inside and occasionally on the outside as well are plastered with mud. Doors and windows are of modern design, made from milled lumber and copied fairly faithfully from the residences of low income white homes. Most of the houses have the traditional hard-packed earth floors characteristic of the old Pueblo homes, but an increasing number of houses have added an innovation—a linoleum floor laid directly over the packed earth. Only one house block in the central courtyard of Hano retains a two-storied terraced structure, formerly a typical architectural feature of the Pueblos. Hano like most of the traditional Hopi villages is still a compact village; however, its houses run parallel to the edge of the cliff with connecting house rows to form a central courtyard or plaza. A kiva, the communal and ceremonial chamber of the Pueblos, is located just off center on the north side of the plaza. Hano has another kiva, a duplicate of the other, outside of the east row of houses and only about fifty feet from the plaza kiva. Both kivas are rectangular, partly underground structures with entrance gained from a ladder protruding from a hatchway in the roof. There is nothing unique about the external appearance of Hano; all of its architectural characteristics may be found in the other Hopi villages.

The Tewa of Hano interact with three categories of people: Hopi, Navaho, and white Americans. The most intensive and intimate relations are with

Hopi neighbors, primarily with those of First Mesa, but schools, herding activities, and ceremonies also bring the Tewa into fairly frequent interaction with the Hopi from more distant villages. Navaho come frequently to trade and attend Hopi and Tewa ceremonies, and those Navaho whose herding territories adjoin those of the Tewa are often encountered on the range or in cattle and sheep camps. Interaction with whites is primarily with government officials and employees, but in the summertime tourists literally invade the Hopi mesas to attend the colorful ceremonies. White missionaries of a number of different Christian denominations are constantly around and the white trader is an important fixture of Hopi and Tewa economy.

Tewa and Hopi Relations

The people of Hano exhibit no difference in general appearance from those of the other Hopi villages. Hano adults are uniformly short or medium statured. Children are so much alike that it is impossible to identify them as Tewa or Hopi. Clothing and hair styles have subtle differences only a Hopi or Tewa can detect, but the old dress styles are fast disappearing as Hopi and Tewa alike take on the dress patterns of white Americans.

The similarity of the two populations is understandable from a biological point of view. There are no marriage restrictions at present; Tewa and Hopi marry freely. Biologically the two populations are now completely mixed, but matrilocal residence, a rule observed by both groups, permits the socio-cultural continuity of the Tewa as a separate unit. Matrilocal residence is a custom that requires the husband to reside with his wife's family in her village. The children of a Tewa or Hopi couple are then raised as members of the wife's family and village, and while the children have intimate and frequent relations with their father and his family, affiliation and primary allegiance is with the mother's family and home.

At Hano, as among the Hopi, women are the important members of the family. They own the land and houses, dispense the food, and make the important decisions. The men perform religious rites, exercise disciplinary powers in their sisters' homes, support their own family, and teach their children "how to make a living," but they have little authority in their own homes and with their own children.

The practices outlined above are inherent in the maternal lineage system which the Hopi and Tewa have. As we shall see in a later section, the reckoning of kin along the maternal line and the custom of matrilocal residence were apparently borrowed from the Hopi, but it is clear that these practices support the Tewa determination to maintain their own society and culture. A Tewa woman never leaves Hano for long; when she marries a Hopi man, he comes to live at Hano and their children are raised as Tewa. If a Hano man marries a Hopi woman, he resides with her in her village, but while his children become Hopi, he himself never loses his Tewa affiliations. Tewa men married to Hopi women consider themselves Tewa and return to Hano to exercise ceremonial and kinship obligations. A Tewa household is impervious to Hopi influence, even in cases of intermarriage. The Hopi husband would find it extremely difficult to impose Hopi values and customs on his children, even if he were disposed to do so. Any attempt at such subversion would be countered by the mother's authority in which the latter would be supported by all the men and women of her maternal lineage.

At the present time about half of the marriages at Hano represent Tewa women married to Hopi men; the other marriages consist of couples where both partners are Tewa. Like Tewa women, approximately half of the married Tewa men have taken Hopi wives. These men reside with their Hopi wives in the latter's natal household. Most of the Tewa-Hopi marriages are with members of the First Mesa villages of Sichomovi and Walpi, but a few have been contracted with Hopi from more distant villages.

Intermarriage with the Hopi in recent years has probably made the Hano more Hopi than Tewa in blood. Yet this knowledge, if the Hopi and the Tewa wonder about it at all, appears to present no anomaly. A Tewa is a person born at Hano of a mother whose maternal lineage runs back unbrokenly to the original Tewa colony. There is no deviation from the rule: "What your mother is you are." A person born of a Tewa father and a Hopi mother is Hopi, not half Tewa and half Hopi; similarly, the child of a Tewa mother, regardless of the father's ethnic affiliation, is Tewa.

Village identity and loyalty are stronger at Hano than among the Hopi who emphasize the maternal kinship or clan bond over village membership. This difference is due in part to the fact that the body of mythological lore is handed down as a village heritage at Hano, rather than as a separate maternal lineage or clan possession as among the Hopi. The Tewa of Hano are staunch supporters and defenders of the cultural heritage of the original Tewa migrants as this body of information has been transmitted and interpreted through time. The most important part of this cultural heritage is an attitude or disposition of the Tewa to preserve their own social and cultural identity. We have noted in the historical section the resistance offered by the ancestors of Hano residents against Spanish oppression in New Mexico and later at Hopi. The struggle continued in their new home, but the resistance has been against social and cultural assimilation with the Hopi. Had the original migrant group been received more graciously they might have been absorbed in a few generations, but it is clear from Hano mythological traditions that the original Tewa group was not welcomed in the manner it wished to be received. Subsequent unfavorable relations between the two groups have produced antagonistic attitudes and negative stereotyping on both sides. Antagonism toward the Hopi is also fed by keeping the migration legend alive. The portion of the legend which tells of the inhospitable reception accorded the original migrant group (see Chapter 2) is recited annually in the Tewa kivas at the time of the Winter Solstice ceremony. In less formal settings, the tale is told in Hano homes on any occasion when feeling against Hopi neighbors runs high. Negative characterizations of the Hopi are also a favorite topic when the Tewa from New Mexico come to visit Hano.

The constant telling of the migration legend has given the Tewa confidence as individuals and reassured them as a group of their special position on First Mesa. The fundamental feature of the legend, the "curse" (see Chapter 2), has been a most effective instrument in keeping the Hopi, particularly those of First Mesa, "in their place." Both groups believe that the prophecy of the tale has been fulfilled: the Hopi do not speak the Tewa language and they know little or nothing about Tewa society and culture. How this was accomplished is not clear, but some reasons can be ventured. The inability of the Hopi to learn the Tewa language in the initial contact period can probably to explained in terms of the numbers involved. The original migrants may have totaled no more than 400 or 500, whereas the Hopi population must have been at least ten times as large. Under these circumstances it would have been easier for the Tewa to learn the Hopi language. This explanation is difficult to accept for the more recent period. Intermarriages with the Hopi and the matrilocal residence custom bring Hopi husbands to live at Hano. It is remarkable that in such unions the Hopi husband does not speak Tewa, even though in many cases he may have spent the major part of his life at Hano and in his Tewa wife's household where Tewa is the preferred language. In such unions the children are, of course, conversant in both languages since husband and wife speak to one another in Hopi and a child must respectfully speak Hopi to his Hopi father, but Tewa to his mother and his Tewa kinfolk at Hano. The Hopi men currently married at Hano do not speak Tewa; most of them surely understand it, but none of them will venture to speak it. To explain this situation one can only point to the strong influence of supernatural sanctions on nonliterate peoples and the attendant development of "psychological sets." So firmly do these people believe in the "curse" that although a Hopi may understand everything said in Tewa he cannot utter a Tewa word.

The Tewa have consciously and consistently tried to maintain a separation from the Hopi in other aspects of their society and culture as well. This behavior is readily understandable. It seems reasonable for a people in a social and numerical minority status to try to retain their own distinctive social and cultural patterns. In this endeavor the Tewa have been highly successful—a success more comprehensible than the provision of the "curse" that prevents the Hopi from speaking Tewa. Specific rituals and social institutions are more tangible than language and their contamination or diffusion can be better controlled.

Why the Tewa migrant group should not have been received with open arms and how subsequently they should have been accorded a minority status is understandable from the Hopi point of view. The Tewa were mercenaries among a people who despise and scorn warriors. To the Hopi religious preoccupation is esteemed and warfare is considered uncouth and barbaric. In the traditions of the Hopi, latecomers were relegated to vulnerable and undesirable points of the mesa in order to meet the brunt of an enemy attack. Early settlers erected their homes in the interior portions of the mesa and when the villages were besieged, they attempted to repel the enemy by prayer retreats in the kivas and by performing magical ceremonies.

The strain on the land resource is another factor that would have placed the incoming Tewa in an unfavorable position. Garden plots had to be found near the mesas because of the constant threat of enemy raids. Good arable land was undoubtedly already appropriated, yet the Tewa had to be accommodated. It is not surprising that antagonisms developed between the two groups.

The social separation of the two societies and mutual ill-feeling throughout most of their contact history is evident in their traditions, but it is apparent in their daily lives as well. For a long time a vacant area existed between Hano and Sichomovi. Although this area was on the Tewa side, no one would build there, and children were afraid to walk over the boundary line into the territory of the other.

While intermarriages are now common, they were forbidden in the past. Marriage restrictions were lifted toward the closing decades of the last century coincident with the establishment of the United States Government Agency at Keams Canyon, the construction of schools, and the advent of white traders. The coming of white Americans brought about a series of changes that altered the former position of the Tewa as a subordinate minority group. We will discuss these interesting changes shortly, but it is important to note other factors that for a long period of time fostered the maintenance of social and cultural separation.

Both groups restricted participation of the other in certain ceremonials. Thus, the Tewa were not permitted in the important Hopi Winter Solstice ceremony at Walpi, and the Hopi were likewise refused admittance to the similar Tewa ceremony. In addition, certain ceremonial benefits were not extended to the other group. For example, at the time of tribal initiation ceremonies in October or November, when priests of participating fraternities came to bless the villages, they stopped at the edge of Sichomovi and did not proceed to Hano. Similarly, Tewa priests during the Winter Solstice ceremony blessed only their portion of First Mesa and did not go to Sichomovi and Walpi.

The Hopi were and are still denied membership in Tewa ceremonial associations despite the reduction of tension between the two groups in recent years. The reason for the restriction is the belief that some dire misfortune will occur if Hopi are permitted membership in Tewa ceremonial associations. The reverse—Tewa joining Hopi associations—is apparently not viewed with such foreboding since Tewa do become members of Hopi ceremonial associations.

Apparently to bolster their own self-importance, the Tewa make repeated references to their special position on First Mesa. They assert that they fulfilled their position as warriors so well that enemy attacks stopped completely. Their roles were then reinterpreted; they became interpreters and "speakers" for the Hopi on First Mesa. That prominent Tewa individuals did indeed operate in these positions is not simply idle boasting. Numerous references are made of Tewa leaders who functioned as spokesmen of the Hopi during the American period. The leader of the delegation which visited James S. Calhoun, the first United States Indian agent of the territory of New Mexico, was a Tewa from Hano. Calhoun spoke of him as the "*cacique* of all the [Hopi] Pueblos." The Indian agent was mistaken, of course; there has never been a "chief" of all the Hopi peoples. Furthermore the term "cacique" could not have been applicable to a Tewa since the term is usually employed among the Pueblos to refer to a religious leader. It is obvious from Calhoun's letter, however, that the man was the spokesman for the group (Calhoun 1915, letter number 82).

An American traveler who visited the Hopi villages in 1872 reports that the Walpi chief on First Mesa had a Tewa interpreter or speaker:

> At [Fort] Defiance I was told to ask for Chino [Cimo or Simo, town chief of Walpi], the *Capitan* of this *mesa* [First Mesa], before I talked to any one else; so I shouted to call out some one. . . . I was greatly relieved when a tall old fellow, with a merry twinkle in his eye, arrived, addressed me in pretty good Spanish, and intimated that he did the talking for Chino when strangers came. His name, which he had on a card written by some white man, was Misiamtewah; he had visited the Mormon settlements and Sante Fe, and could speak Spanish, Moqui [Hopi], Tegua and a little English and Navajo, besides being fluent in the sign language. I cultivated his acquaintance at once. (Beadle 1878:266–267)

About the turn of the century Tom Polacca, for whom the village at the foot of First Mesa is named, served as interpreter and speaker. Polacca learned to speak English and represented the Hopi in important conferences, accompanying in 1890 a delegation of Hopi chiefs to Washington D.C. in order to present the needs of the Hopi personally to the Indian commissioner.

During the time of my field studies, the official Hopi interpreter was Albert Yava, a Tewa Indian. The following incident indicates the importance of the Tewa interpreter on First Mesa. On one occasion, during this period, the superintendent of the Hopi Agency arranged a meeting at Walpi. He was not able to find Yava so he brought along a very able Hopi Indian interpreter to the meeting. The Hopi refused flatly to go on with the meeting unless the Tewa interpreter could be secured. The superintendent complied, but it was very late at night before he located Yava and the meeting could be resumed.

In other roles involving meetings with outsiders, or in fulfilling responsible positions distasteful to the Hopi, the Tewa have been pressed into service. The positions of policemen, for example, have also devolved to the Tewa. Leo Crane, a government Indian agent for the Hopi from 1911 to 1919, comments on Tewa policemen and makes some discerning remarks about Hopi and Tewa personality differences:

> The Hopi do not make good policemen, and certainly not in a cohort of one. Their very name implies "the peaceful ones." Their towns are ruled largely by pueblo opinion. If a resident acquires the reputation of being unreasonable and unfeeling, as a policeman often must, his standing in the outraged community may affect all other phases of his life. Therefore the Hopi is not likely to become a very zealous officer when operating alone. And too, the Hopi fear the Navajo, as it is said the Navajo fear the Ute, and are useless when removed from the neighborhood of their homes.
>
> But many years ago, when the Hopi were sorely pressed by nomad enemies and had not even the consolation of telling their woes to an Indian Agent, they sent emissaries to their cousins, the Pueblo Indians of what is now New Mexico, and begged for a colony of warriors to reside with them. In response to this plea, and looking for something to their advantage, in 1700 came a

band of Tewa. . . . To these people the Hopi granted a wide valley west of the First Mesa, known as the Wepo Wash, providing they would stay and lend their prowess in future campaigns. They built a village atop the First Mesa, now called Tewa or Hano, where their descendants live today. Some intermarried with Hopi, and a few with nearby Navajo; but they have not been absorbed, and it is a curious fact that while all the Tewa speak Hopi and Navajo with more or less fluency, after two centuries of living side by side few of the Hopi can speak the Tewa dialect.

The Hopi invited warriors, and the warriors have graduated into policemen, for one learns to police the Hopi districts, and even to discipline some of the Navajo, with Tewa officers. They are dependable and courageous, even belligerent; that is to say, they will fight when it is necessary and, strange thing among desert Indians, with their fists, taking a delight in blacking the opponent's eye. But one has to learn that the Hopi as policemen are fine ceremonial dancers. (Crane 1925:136–137)

Crane's astute observations of Hopi character was underscored by Solomon Asch who made a field study of Hopi attitudes in the 1940s:

All individuals must be treated alike; no one must be superior and no one must be inferior. The person who is praised or who praises himself is automatically subject to resentment and to criticism, the object of which is to bring him back into the slow, hard-plodding line of all Hopi. . . .

Most Hopi men refuse to be foremen on jobs which the government sponsors on the reservation. If they do, they are immediately accused of thinking they are better than others, and are continually badgered by disparaging remarks. For example, P., an able, hard-working fellow, excels on the job and is frequently given the position of foreman, which he accepts. He is very unpopular. . . . A more telling bit of evidence is that they do not compare the importance of one another's work. A highly skilled stone-cutter is perfectly content to accept the same wages as an unskilled day laborer. (Asch, in manuscript)

First Mesa Hopi have found the Tewa willing to perform the tasks which the Hopi disdain. The Tewa, on the other hand, have been content to do them for the occasional morsel of approval and appreciation they receive from their neighbors. As one Tewa put it: "We are criticized and ridiculed for whatever we do so why not perform the work that needs to be done?" Primary reinforcement for anti-Hopi behavior comes from their own community where aggressive and individualized behavior is valued. In recent years approval has come from another source: white Americans endorse the outgoing personality characteristics of the Tewa. Government officials and whites generally have praised the "progressive" Tewa and pointed to them as models of the "proper attitude" Indians should have in the modern world. In the 1880s Julian Scott, a special agent for the Hopi tribe remarked: "They [the Tewa] show a pronounced difference in their bearing from the pure Moqui [Hopi]. . . . They are foremost in all things that pertain to their future good, and were the first to leave the mesa and build new homes more convenient to wood and water and their fields." (U.S. Dept. Int. 1894: 190). Actually the Tewa are bound to their mesa homes as much as the Hopi. Many Tewa built additional homes below the mesa, but Hano is still a thriving community. Scott's observation on the differences in "bearing" between Hopi and Tewa, however, has been noted by many other visitors to Hano and the Hopi villages.

Two prominent Tewa highlight the individualized behavior valued by whites and Tewa alike. One is Tom Polacca already mentioned as the official interpreter of First Mesa in the 1890s; the other is Nampeyo, a Tewa woman potter. Polacca became a prosperous livestock owner and built a large house at the foot of the mesa about the beginning of the century. It was around this nucleus that the present town of Polacca was built. Polacca's influence was so strong with United States governmental officials that he was proposed by the government agent in 1891 to succeed the deceased town chief of Walpi. Since this position is a religious office and is hereditary within the Hopi Bear clan or its linked clans, the Hopi protested bitterly and were able to dissuade the agent from actually forcing Polacca into the position. The incident, however, is indicative of the man's prestige with government authorities.

Before the Spanish period pottery manufacture was an important occupation in all of the Hopi villages. The craft died out completely after the first century of Spanish rule. Some say that this was because pottery, as the chief article of tribute, was so identified with Spanish oppression that the Hopi stopped making it because it reminded them of that period of suffering. But the Hopi, at least those of First Mesa, were ready for its revival at the beginning of the century. The person who brought about the renaisssance of pottery making was a Tewa woman, Nampeyo. This woman studied the pottery excavated by an archeologist in the nearby ruins of Sikyatki, experimented with clay ingredients and firing and copied the old pottery designs. Finally she succeeded; her product had an individuality of its own, but it is just as vital and attractive as the pottery of the ancient Hopi of Sikyatki. Because of its economic importance, revitalized pottery manufacture soon spread to Sichomovi and Walpi and is now the basic craft of First Mesa.

Polacca and Nampeyo shared one important characteristic: they were both traditional Tewa, participating in the ceremonies, working parties, and food exchanges of the community. In this respect Polacca and Nampeyo were little different from other Tewa, and they were not considered to be deviants or outstanding persons by the inhabitants of Hano. The fame of these two is due almost completely to their popularization by American friends. Polacca and Nampeyo, in adhering to the traditional pattern of life, became submerged as individuals in the society. The fruit of their economic success was shared, however, by all the inhabitants of First Mesa through the system of exchange of food and services.

It is clear at present that the attitudes of hostility and antagonism discussed earlier in this section are being ameliorated. For example, resistance to the Hopi way of life is stronger with the older Tewa. At the Winter Solstice ceremony it is old men who emphasize that the Tewa must not forget Hopi injustices. Young people have much in common with the Hopi, and they tend to minimize and even laugh off these serious admonitions. Consequently, old legends tend to disappear with the passing of the aged, and young Tewa seem content to forget them. Reduced friction between the two groups in recent years seems to be directly related to white contact. The unfavorable position of the Tewa on First Mesa induced them to cooperate more readily with whites. As a result of this cooperation the Tewa became acquainted with the techniques of livestock raising and wage work. The revival of pottery making, as we have noted, started at Hano and diffused to the Hopi. Tewa successes with these new economic activities brought about reduced tensions and emulation from their Hopi neighbors on First Mesa, which in turn paved the way to greater interdependence and cooperation, particularly in social and secular activities.

A reconstruction of events as they must have happened may be briefly stated. The original Tewa group came into the profoundly religiously oriented Hopi society. The Tewa religious repertoire was less complex than the Hopi and it emphasized curing (see Chapter 5) rather than "weather control." Tewa religion was also more secular because of a politically oriented social organization (see Chapter 4) and a hundred years of Spanish influence. As newcomers, the Tewa were assigned the role of "protectors" in the traditional Hopi manner. To a religion concerned primarily with "weather control" through ritual the Tewa had little to contribute. Their curing societies may have been welcome, but they probably had no important ceremonies to appease the harsh environment. Skill as warriors was helpful, but war was despicable to the Hopi and was not a prestige-bearing activity. If the Tewa displayed the outgoing, aggressive personalities that characterize their present descendants, they were probably even less desired, for Hopi behavior is ideally passive.

Tewa values at Hopi must have taken literally a "back seat." The Hopi no doubt had little respect for this religiously poverty-stricken society. They did "use" the ancestors of the Tewa, however, in the roles that they disdained—the prestigeless positions of warriors, and later as interpreters and go-betweens. In an attempt to assert their own self-importance, the Tewa accused the Hopi of inhospitality and ungracious behavior. They bolstered their own group ego by remaining aloof, reiterating Hopi injustices, and extolling their own virtues as warriors and emissaries.

White American contact altered the value system in favor of the Tewa. Americans like the Tewa are "practical," and the aggressive and outgoing personality of the Tewa is remarkably "American." The Tewa readily and enthusiastically took to stock-raising, wage work and the white man's schools. Their children, already trained in two languages, learned English more quickly than the Hopis. Moreover, their greater motivation as a minority spurred them to excel in the classroom. In the process, the Hopi began to develop a new respect for the Tewa. The Tewa role as emissaries and interpreters to the white people grew in importance and prestige. Their value orientation, remarkably like that of the newcomers, no longer had to take a back seat. The Hopi saw that "it paid to be like the whites," and the Tewa were providing the lead to this new and positive achievement.

The Tewa have thus exerted considerable influence on First Mesa, which has diffused in weaker currents to other Hopi villages. Today there is constant interaction and cooperation between the two populations on First Mesa. Intermarriages and the acquisition of relatives on both sides have intricately related all of the people. The "healthy social climate" and a generally cooperative atmosphere with the government and outsiders, noted on First Mesa by various investigators, is attributable largely to the Tewa. (See Thompson 1950: 78–80)

Relations with Navaho and Other Indians

The Navaho have been neighbors of the Hopi villages for a long time. About 200 years prior to their removal to eastern New Mexico they constantly raided and plundered Hopi fields and threatened the lives of the villagers (Chapter 2). The Tewa and Hopi enjoyed a brief respite from the Navaho menace, but a few years after being returned to their native land, problems with the Navaho again appeared. This time Navaho cattle and sheep herds encroached on Tewa and Hopi lands. Bitter relations developed as the Hopi reservation was reduced to only about one-fourth of the area designated in the original executive order. Increase in landholdings for the rapidly increasing Navaho population was thus at the expense of the Hopi and Tewa economic activity in horticulture and livestock. These problems brought about a reconsideration of the executive order that established the Hopi reservation. The boundary dispute has not yet been settled, and at this writing it is still being argued in the courts.

Despite these difficulties, face to face contacts between the Tewa and the Navaho are usually pleasant, and visiting and trading relations have been a well-established pattern for at least a half century. During the summer, in cattle and sheep camps, prolonged social contacts with neighboring Navaho families are maintained. There is, as well, frequent attendance at one another's ceremonies. From such associations many Tewa have acquired great facility with the Navaho language. These contacts have also provided opportunity to learn Navaho songs and ceremonies as well as to make the observations necessary for burlesquing Navahos in the winter kiva dances. A form of the *Yeibichai*—part of the Navaho Night Way—is performed every winter as one of the series of night kachina dances.

Many Navaho in the lower economic levels spend weeks or even months moving from one ceremonial celebration in one part of the Navaho reservation to another. Often these Navaho include the Hopi villages and Hano on their visiting cycle. The Tewa welcome these "vagabonds," as they refer to them, but treat them condescendingly. While the best eating and sleeping accommodations are provided for visiting Pueblo Indians, these Navaho are often made to eat on the floor separately from their hosts and to sleep outdoors.

Inter-Indian affairs like the Gallup Intertribal Ceremonial and the Flagstaff Pow-wow are also bringing Tewa and Hopi Indians in contact with other Indians. More and more Tewa and Hopi now visit the Rio Grande Pueblos and meet other Indians in the urban centers of Albuquerque, Santa Fe, Gallup, and Phoenix. As the result of these contacts, a number of intermarriages have taken place. The non-Tewa, non-Hopi spouse sometimes comes to the Hopi reservation to live, but the more typical pattern is for the couple to move into an off-reservation town and for the husband to take up unskilled or semi-skilled wage work. These movements are adding a significant Indian population to off-reservation towns.

The participation of Tewa and Hopi individuals in this network of inter-Indian relations is an important stimulus to acculturation. There are greater opportunities today for the exchange of ideas and information that affect not only the groups living away from the reservation, but which also filter back to the mesa communities. Despite the efforts of the Tewa and Hopi to insulate their communities against the introduction of alien practices and ideas, these influences are modifying the traditional way of life.

Relations with Whites

The Tewa, like their Hopi neighbors, tend to separate whites into three groups: missionaries, tourists, and agency personnel. In the last category, teachers, agency employees, and medical people are all lumped together. The white trader does not fit into any of these groups. He has a personal relationship to the Indians. He is a link, primarily economic, with the outside world.

Missionaries

Missionaries are primarily members of Protestant denominations. Catholic missionaries have not been successful among the Hopi and Tewa, perhaps because of the word-of-mouth tales of the ill-treatment accorded their forefathers by Spanish priests. During my fieldwork period, the following missions were on the Hopi reservation: three Baptist missions, at Polacca, Toreva (below Second Mesa), and Keams Canyon; two Mennonite missions, at Oraibi and Bakabi; a Roman Catholic Franciscan mission at Keams Canyon serving primarily Navahos; and a Protestant mission of undetermined affiliation at Sichomovi, conducted by a native Hopi missionary. In addition to these missions, missionaries and representatives of other Protestant sects visit the Hopi villages periodically. These people hold services in Hopi and Tewa homes or simply read the Bible and sing hymns, coaxing members of the household to join in. Some Tewa women appear to enjoy the singing, but none of them participate in the services wholeheartedly.

Most of the missionaries who visit the Hopi or who have missions on the Hopi reservation disapprove of the Hopi and Tewa ceremonies. Some of the sects vehemently denounce the traditonal customs and instruct their Hopi and Tewa adherents to abandon them. The Indians attend church services or Bible readings primarily to receive the gifts and nonreligious instruction which are offered as inducements to come to the missions. One woman said she had learned to sew and to can fruit by attending the services of one sect and valued this knowledge. It is obvious that few of the Hopi or the Tewa have found spiritual satisfaction in their exposure to Christian teaching. Pueblo Indians are concerned about the problems of daily living and seek to find relief from illness, crop failure, and difficulties with Indian and white neighbors. Their own religion is organized to minimize the fears and anxieties of day to day existence. They cannot understand a religion that emphasizes the spiritual world. Sin and "being saved" are concepts that are simply not a part of their thinking. They do not believe that their ancestors have wronged anyone and hence they have no "guilt", in the sense that whites have it. But they do have apprehensions about the contemporary world and are seeking relief from them. Hopi and Tewa ceremonies, particularly those of the Hopi, are mass magical rites with an emphasis on beauty of movement and costuming. They are designed and executed to induce the universe to pour forth with the good things of life. Horticulture, the economic base of life, receives the full concentration of Hopi religious devotion and ritual. In an environment where the success or failure of the subsistence economy is always fraught with uncertainty, the religious orientation of the longer term residents like the Hopi highlights "weather control." Lean and bountiful years are explained in terms of faulty or successful observance of religious retreats and rituals.

Christianity has no solutions for such concerns or problems.

While the Tewa have a more secular orientation, their religious organization, ritual, and beliefs are closer to the Hopi than to any Christian sect. They have resisted the inroads of Christianity, particularly in the early years of forceful imposition, just as strongly and persistently as have the Hopi.

In the early 1900s the ceremonies of the Hopi, the Tewa, and other Western Indians came under severe criticism. The United States government sent investigators to study reports of immoral and anti-Christian practices among the Indians. These investigators brought back reports of customs that violated white American standards of decency and morality. Under the religious Crimes Code, Indian Service officials were instructed to stop ceremonial practices that might be contrary to accepted Christian standards. The impending suppression of native ceremonial rites caused the Hopi, the Tewa, and the Pueblos of New Mexico to entrench their native ceremonial system. The situation was like a return to the days of Spanish oppression and the Pueblos survived this period of religious persecution by the same method—by holding their ceremonies behind closed doors and disciplining themselves to reveal no information about their sacred rites to outsiders.

The Hopi and Tewa are masters at passive resistance. Numerically small and unacquainted with the legal techniques with which to fight injustices, they resist by hiding behind a wall of secrecy. Elsie Clews Parsons, an anthropologist, who edited a fascinating personal journal of a Tewa Indian (Crow-wing) remarks in her foreword to the journal:

> That missionaries should come up the mesa into the plazas is greatly resented, . . . and some have wanted to put them out, forcibly, as a missionary was treated at Oraibi, tossed in a blanket, I was told with a grim laugh. But

others, among them our Journalist, have counselled the pose of indifference, of suppressing by ignoring. 'Let them alone, have nothing to do with them, don't speak to them,' he advises, as determined an exponent of passive resistance as might once have been found, let us say in Germany. Even in the Journal, Crow-wing carries out his policy. Not a word about the missionaries. They are negligible and ignored. (Parsons 1925:8)

Fortunately in the early 1920s the U.S. Indian Bureau reversed itself and stressed the right of Indians to practice their own religion. The suppression of ceremonies has had a negative effect on the spread of Christianity among the Hopi and Tewa. Christian missionaries today are identified by many of the people with the onus of religious persecution. The Tewa, however, do not seem to consider the missionaries at present a serious threat to their way of life and they express no particular hostility toward them. Missionaries are received courteously in the homes of many Tewa, but the attitude toward their missionary activities is one of polite tolerance. A Tewa woman expressed in words what might be witnessed by any impartial observer:

It is best to be polite to missionaries, let them come in and preach. We will go on with what we are doing. It is not good to drive anyone away; we must be nice to people no matter who they are. But we feel that no one should disturb what we want to do. If they urge us to listen, we say nothing. Sometimes they talk a long time telling us that our dances are evil and that we must stop them. They say unless we go the "Christian Road" we will not be saved. But we just keep quiet and they get tired after a while and leave us alone.

Traders

The white trader has been an important part of the Hopi and Tewa scene since the late decades of the last century. Traders have the opportunity to acquire an intimate knowledge of the Indians rarely available to non-Indians. While the relationship is primarily an economic one, many traders have taken a personal interest in the mesa communities. Thomas V. Keam, a trader of the Hopi and Navaho, for whom Keams Canyon was named, became intimately involved in the problems of the Hopi and the Tewa. It was through his efforts that the delegation of Hopi chiefs made the trip to visit the Commissioner of Indian Affairs in 1890 to Washington, D.C., to present personally the problems of the Hopi Indians (see this Chapter, p. 27).

In 1951 white traders operated three trading posts where the Tewa did most of their buying. One trader operated two large posts, one at Polacca and one in Keams Canyon. A second trading post in Keams Canyon was perhaps most popular with the Tewa. The owner of this post, a white man, had a Tewa clerk who handled most of the sales to Tewa and Hopi customers. Prices are extremely high in the trading posts, but it is a convenient way to buy, and many Indians have charge accounts of long standing in these places. The traders are generally held in higher esteem than missionaries or many of the Indian Service personnel since traders do not try to persuade them to change their way of life.

Tourists

During the summer, and less frequently at other times, hundreds of tourists come to visit the Hopi villages and Hano. Non-Indian visitors are drawn by the unusual beauty of the mesa country and also by the esoteric and colorful ceremonies. The visits of tourists are usually transient and of short duration, but there are numerous instances of a casual first visit developing into an enduring friendship between an individual Tewa or Hopi family and a family from a distant part of the country. Such friendships stimulate repeated visits. These friends are frequently drawn into taking the side of their Indian friends in petty disputes within the community, a practice that has often aggravated the trouble rather than helped matters. In a few instances, however, these friends have helped the Indians tremendously in problems that affected them all. Thus, the friends of the Indians, particularly artists and writers, joined the Indians in fighting the suppression of native customs and ceremonies and in winning for the Indians the right to hold them.

The Tewa have coined a special term for whites who come to see their ceremonies and appear to enjoy them. They are called "unbaptized" ones to differentiate them from missionaries and other whites who have denounced their customs and ceremonies. There is no resentment toward white visitors at either Tewa or Hopi dances. Both groups feel that all share in bringing about good, the spectators as well as the dancers. Hence, as long as tourists are well behaved they are welcome. Yet, photographs of public ceremonial performances are prohibited, for the Tewa and Hopi fear that such pictures may still be used to subvert and suppress their religious activities.

United States Indian Service

The Bureau of Indian Affairs has probably affected the Tewa and Hopi more profoundly than any other source of change. Before the mid-twenties, Indian administration was committed to transforming Indian communities into variants of the dominant American culture as quickly as possible. We have noted the critical attitude of missionaries and U.S. Indian Service officials toward native Indian mores and their attempts to stop them. Indian administrators also used force in recruiting Indian children to be enrolled in boarding schools located in the eastern part of the United States. The program was designed specifically to wean Indian youngsters from their traditional culture. In these schools the use of the Indian language and all other "Indian" ways were prohibited. Infractions were dealt with brutally through a variety of physical punishments. Tewa and Hopi children were among the many Indian children affected by these activities of the Bureau of Indian Affairs.

Criticism of the Indian Bureau's policy was strong and it succeeded, as we have seen, in securing for the people the right to hold their own ceremonies.

In addition, exposure of the abuses of the earlier period brought about a change in policy. After 1928 the Bureau respected the Indian ways of life, but assisted them in improving their economic, educational, and health problems. The new regime has permitted traditional Tewa and Hopi leaders to relax controls that safeguard their ceremonial life. But they *have not abandoned* these controls; the bitter experience of two periods of religious persecution is deeply imbedded in their memory. Insistence upon the preservation of a distinctive way of life has been dramatically illustrated by the Hano Tewa, but in general, cultural self-determination is an American Indian characteristic, if indeed it is not a universal human trait.

Since the late nineteenth century, the Tewa have felt the value of cooperating with government representatives and with white people in general. These relationships have had for the most part a positive effect on Tewa culture, but certain disintegrating factors are also emerging as a result of increasing contacts with Americans and American institutions. Thus, for example, a serious incompatibility is evident between the younger, school-trained generation and the older, traditionally reared group. Off-reservation boarding schools are blamed by the Tewa for this situation. Young dissidents consist mainly of youths from seventeen to twenty-five who loiter in the trading posts and at favorite spots along the protecting eaves of the cliffs on First Mesa. Sometimes girls are drawn into the group but for the most part they are youths from First Mesa ranging in number from twenty to twenty-five—although only about six to ten ever congregate together at any one time. These are the young people who take to drinking and often get into trouble and then must appear before the tribal judge at Keams Canyon. Drinking is not a serious problem at present, however; the fact that liquor must be bought in off-reservation towns and brought seventy-five miles to the Hopi mesas has undoubtedly restricted heavy and habitual drinking. In addition, the rich ceremonial cycle provides sufficient satisfactions to discourage the use of liquor as a substitute for recreational outlets.

Not all of the young people with formal education are die-hard iconoclasts; family and community pressures bring many of them to participate in traditional activities. Still, the attitude of many young people is to look with disfavor on Hopi and Tewa ceremonies and to make carping criticisms of Hopi and Tewa life. The traditionalists feel that anyone who rejects native customs is "bad" and "mean." To effect conformity, scolding and community pressures are employed. The result is greater resentment on the part of the small but increasing group of young dissidents and a widening of the gap of misunderstanding between them and the traditionalists. The group may represent simply the usual, general differences to be found in any community; yet with Tewa and Hopi culture, nonconformance to traditional customs does signal the passing of a unique way of life since ceremonial participation is such a vital part of the social order. It would be ironic that the Tewa of Hano after resisting the corrosive and acculturative pressures of a number of different societies over such a long span of history should finally succumb to the influences of white American culture.

The Yearly Round of Activities

While the ceremonies and customs at Hano may disappear in a few generations, Tewa culture at present exhibits considerable vitality. During the winter months the ceremonial calendar is full, and cooperative activities (see Chapter 6) of all kinds bring the people together. With the harvest carefully stored away and the work of herding cattle and sheep reduced to a minimum, most of the Tewa families come back to Hano to spend the winter. Kiva dances occur weekly; in between times there are continuous rehearsals for men, while Tewa women are occupied with the preparation of food.

The winter months are the time for constant social interaction. There is visiting in the evening; stories are told and experiences recounted. Most of the talk and activities, however, center around the kiva dances; the last performances are discussed while the next one is planned and eagerly anticipated.

Early in the spring the ceremonial cycle wanes. Planning and work with sheep and cattle keep entire families away from the mesa. There are only two major ceremonies in the summertime—the Niman Kachina and the Snake Dance (or Flute Dance in alternate years). Both of these are First Mesa Hopi ceremonies, and while the Tewa do not actively participate in them, they must prepare food for their Hopi relatives gained through intermarriage. The Tewa also act as hosts to outside visitors since, in recent years, they are considered and therefore consider themselves members of First Mesa society. For these important summer events families that have been away in cattle and sheep camps return, but for only a few days. As soon as the ceremonies are over they are back at work. These two ceremonies, however, are eagerly anticipated, and they provide considerable social interaction not only among themselves but with hundreds of visitors—whites, Navaho, and Pueblo Indians.

Families living at Keams Canyon, the Hopi Agency, participate in recreational activities supplied by government supervisors and Christian missions. These consist of periodic American social dances, basketball games, and weekly movies. The Baptist church conducts a weekly sewing class, which draws a small group of irregular participants. But even these people seem to find the social interaction, ceremonies, and cooperative activities on top of the mesa more satisfying. Since the winter Kachina dances now occur regularly on Saturday nights, a concession made specifically for wage workers, some of the Tewa families living on job locations in Holbrook, Winslow, and Flagstaff also come to see them from time to time. The sacrifices that these people make to attend Tewa ceremonies and renew kinship ties are indicative of the strength of traditional Tewa culture.

For the present, Tewa society and culture persist. With the coming of white Americans a more amicable and cooperative atmosphere has been established on First Mesa which offsets the former antagonistic relations between the Hopi and Tewa. American contact has acted as a catalyst in the change by altering the value system in favor of the Tewa. Basic Hopi and Tewa social institutions and practices have not been displaced and remain strong and satisfying to the people. Social cohesion on First Mesa seems to have been achieved without leveling differences and without seriously undermining the traditional cultural core on which each society rests. Modifications brought about by modern conditions are evident, but despite these changes the vitality of Hano continues. In the chapters that follow we will examine in some detail the customs and institutions of the Tewa community.

4

The Social Network

To THE ORDINARY AMERICAN TOURIST on a casual visit to Hano and the Hopi villages, the differences in social life from the general American pattern may not be immediately apparent. Accustomed to his society where descent is reckoned bilaterally with an emphasis on the male line, he will naturally assume that the same conditions exist at Hano and among the Hopi. It is only after greater familiarity with the social relations and the social organizations of these people that he will be impressed by striking differences. The tourist will then begin to realize that the way in which he groups relatives and the way he regards and behaves toward his relatives and neighbors is as alien to the Tewa of Hano as the social life of Hano will be to him.

The Hano kinship system is based on unilateral descent, and the social structures given prominence in Hano life are also unilateral organizations. These units are the matrilineal, extended household, the lineage, and the clan. The nuclear or elementary family which is the basic family type in American society is a temporary unit among the Tewa and the result of acculturation to white American influences. Only the Tewa living off the mesa on cattle and sheep camps or those engaged in wage work in urban areas outside of the Hopi reservation live in nuclear families. The family organization at Hano is an extended type where relatives related along the maternal line live in rooms and houses adjacent to one another. Married men live with their wives, but look upon the households of their mothers and sisters as their real homes. These men return frequently to their natal households to participate in ceremonial life and to exercise their authority over junior members of their own lineages. Hano households are the terminal structures of a number of matrilineal lineages which in turn form the important clan structures. One household in each clan is the custodian of the ceremonial lore and the religious paraphernalia of the clan. The oldest woman of this household is the head of the clan, but the "real" clan leader is her brother or perhaps a maternal uncle. This man performs rituals periodically for the benefit of all clan members and as such he is held in high esteem.

The kinship system and the lineal structures are the most significant aspects of the Hano social system. These organizations are similar to Hopi counterparts, and the Tewa must have adjusted their own institutions with those of their neighbors early in the contact period. At present the survival of Hano Tewa culture depends primarily on the continuity of these institutions.

The Household

Kinship relations at Hano may be comprehended most easily by a discussion of the extended matrilineal household where an individual receives his initial and basic cultural orientation. This unit normally consists of a woman and her husband, married daughters and their husbands, unmarried sons, and children of the daughters. The women comprise the important members of the unit; they own the house, are responsible for the preparation and distribution of food, make all the important decisions, and care for the religious paraphernalia. The oldest woman of the household enjoys the most respect, and the members of the unit look to her for instructions and seek her advice in times of trouble. Next in importance is her oldest daughter, who assumes the duties and responsibilities of the household in the absence of her mother. Men of the household and lineage leave the house when they marry, although they return frequently, consider it their home, exercise considerable authority in religious matters, and are called to exert discipline over the children in serious cases. The husbands have little authority in the wife's home; they contribute to its economic support, teach their children the techniques of making a livelihood, and provide warmth and real affection toward them but defer to their wives and their wives' brothers and uncles in disciplinary matters.

The extended household formerly occupied a series of adjacent rooms. With the increasing importance of wage work and livestock activities in recent years, this situation has changed. Tewa families on farms and ranches during the summer are essentially of the nuclear-family type: husband, wife, and children, and in some cases, a widowed grandmother, a divorced daughter, or other relative and her children are present. For wage workers, housing limitations at Keams Canyon or off the reservation restrict the size of the household even more drastically. Although it is not uncommon to have one or even both parents of the wife living with a nuclear family on a farm or ranch, older people refuse to make their home with children who live in government quarters or off the reservation.

At Polacca and Hano the size and composition of the households vary seasonally and with the occurrence of ceremonial and social functions. During these events the households are considerably larger. Hano individuals consider the residences on farms or ranches, at Keams Canyon, or off the reservation as temporary and retain homes at Tewa Village or Polacca. Here they return frequently for various social and ceremonial occasions and revert to extended-household living. The structure and activities of a typical Tewa household are discussed in Chapter 6.

The household in recent years has thus tended to become a less integrated unit than it was formerly; nevertheless there is keen awareness of all the relatives that comprise the household group. Modern forms of transportation afford frequent resumptions of extended-household living. The growing child still has a maximum of contact with a large number of relatives. A child soon learns to identify grandparents, parents, his mother's sisters and their husbands and children, and his own brothers and sisters. For much of the time he eats, sleeps, and plays in the company of these relatives.

Almost· simultaneously with his contact with the relatives of the household group, though not with the same frequency, the child comes into contact with his father's relatives. These relatives, particularly father's mother and father's sisters, are frequent visitors to his house, and he is always welcome and treated with affection in their house. At crucial periods of his life they comfort and aid him. Thus, for example, when the *Soyoku* (bogey Kachina, see Social Control below) come at the time of the *Powamu* ceremony, these relatives intercede for him and prevent the frightening ogres from carrying him away.

The enculturation process will become more evident in the discussion of kinship behavior and the life cycle, but the initial indoctrination of a Tewa individual cannot be thoroughly understood unless the structural makeup of the household is comprehended.

Lineage and Clan

A Hano lineage is the living and functional representation of a particular clan; its members are in intimate contact with one another and bound together by deep loyalties. While marriages remove the men to the various households of their wives, they renew lineage ties frequently to exercise ceremonial responsibilities. Women of the lineage are, of course, constantly together. The lineages at Hano are small and some are simply the matrilineal members of an extended household. A senior woman of one of the lineages is the head of the clan and her brother ordinarily performs the necessary rituals for the clan. Upon the death of the clan head, the position is usually assumed by the next senior woman of the same household and lineage, but prominent members of the clan in the village may decide to designate as her successor a mature woman from another household and lineage. Formerly households of the lineage occupied a block of houses adjacent to one another, a pattern that has broken down in recent years, but the intimate kinship bond remains even though the member household may be dispersed. Since the Tewa recognize affiliation with Hopi clans having the same name, lineages of equivalent clans in the Hopi villages are also considered lineal kinfolk and the ordinary clan relations are extended to members of these lineages.

Hano lineages and clans resemble corresponding Hopi organizations in all essential features. Certain basic Hopi concepts, particularly those concerned with phratral groupings and separate clan migration legends, appear to be new to the Tewa.[1] In recent years, however, there is clearly an indication that the Tewa

---

[1] See below for a discussion of Hopi and Hano phratry organization.

are attempting to adapt and adjust their own clan concepts to correspond with those of the Hopi. These efforts of the Tewa to accommodate to Hopi clan concepts disclose subtle but important factors in the trend toward acculturation noted in Chapter 3 and discussed in this and in the following sections.

Characteristics of Hano clan organization are revealed in the following statement by a Bear clansman:

> I am of the Bear clan. Our mothers' mothers' mothers and our mothers' mothers' mothers' brothers were Bear clan people. They came a long, long, time ago from *Tsawadeh*, our home in the east. Our sisters' daughters' daughters' children, as long as women of my clan have children, will be of the Bear clan. These are our clan relatives, whom we trust, work with, and confide in. My mother's older sister guards the sacred fetish which is the power and guardian of our clan and which was brought in the migration from *Tsawadeh*. My mother's older sister feeds our fetish and sees that the feathers are always properly dressed. At important ceremonies, my mother's brother, erects his altar and sets our fetish in a prominent place within the altar. My mother's older sister and my mother's brother make all the important decisions for our clan, and such decisions are accepted with respect and obedience by all Bear clan members. My mother's older sister and her brother are called upon to advise, to reprimand, and to make decisions on land and ritual affairs for all of us who are of the Bear clan. My mother's older sister's house is where our fetish is kept, and therefore it is a sacred house to us and there we go for all important matters that concern our clan.

A few additional remarks about the nature of the Tewa clan are necessary to complete the above description. Marriage between members of the same clan are strictly prohibited. In addition, marriage is forbidden with a member of an equivalent Hopi, New Mexico Pueblo, or Navaho clan; a member of father's clan or of its linked clans; and a person whose father's clan is the same as one's own. Occasionally violations of these latter restrictions have occurred, but no violation of the rule that forbids marriage with a member of one's own clan is on record at Hano.

Clans are landholding units, each clan having lands set aside for the use of its members. The control of ceremonies and their ritual paraphernalia are in the keeping of certain clans. Adopted children retain the clan of their mothers; in all cases of adoption at Hano, however, the children were adopted by members of their own clan.

The importance of the matrilineal clan among the Hano can only be attributed to borrowing from the Hopi, for the New Mexico Tewa do not have a functional clan organization. These Pueblos group themselves into "clan" names but these units have neither function nor clearly defined patterns of descent and residence. These "clans" have nothing to do with ceremonial or economic affairs, land or house control, political organization, or the regulation of marriage. New Mexico Tewa Indians report variously that one acquires such a "clan" from the father or the mother. It appears then that, among the New Mexico Tewa at least, the borrowing of the clan from some diffusing agents—

perhaps from their Keresan neighbors who have clans of the Hopi type—was arrested before it became a significant part of their social organization. Possibly Spanish influences acted as a deterrent to the diffusion of clan concepts, particularly since the Spanish colonists were strongly patrilineal. At any rate, only "clan names" exist among the New Mexico Tewa at present, and it is very probable that the migrant Tewa group at Hopi had a similar undeveloped clan organization. The idea of the clan was not foreign, however, and it is possible that this nuclear idea was developed quite early into an organization which approximated the Hopi clan. An early adaptation of the kinship and clan organizations would have facilitated the preservation of a distinctive way of life, which, as the present study indicates, the ancestors of the Tewa desired. Hopi kinship and clan organizations stress matrilineal descent and matrilocal residence, hence it is possible to isolate an intermarrying community from others if its members wanted to be alone. Hano did, in fact, maintain a separation from the Hopi for over two centuries, and, as we have noted, only in comparatively recent times have intermarriages occurred and the trend toward an integrated Hopi and Tewa community on First Mesa launched.

New Mexico Tewa visitors are fully conscious of the importance of the clan among the Hopi and at Hano. They have learned from experience, for instance, that they receive more cordial treatment in the homes of Hano Tewa whose clan corresponds to their "name clan" than they do from others; therefore they proudly announce their "clan" as soon as they arrive at Hano. A New Mexico Tewa visitor is asked: "What clan are you?" When identity is established, the visitor is supposed to stay with his clan relatives. If the Tewa visitor gives the name of a clan not represented at Hano, the answer invariably is: "They have become extinct." Hano residents believe that at one time the village had a full complement of all Tewa clans, and if the "clan name" of a Tewa visitor cannot be identified, the clan must be extinct. In the event that a clan is not found for a Tewa visitor, any Hano household will take him in and treat him with kindness and respect, just as he would be treated if he were a real member of that household and clan.

The Hano clan has apparently mirrored the Hopi clan in structure and function for a long time, but the principle of clan linkage or phratry organization appears to be new to the Tewa. Among the Hopi, all the clans are grouped into larger aggregates of phratries of two or more clans each. Eggan (1950, Table 2, pp. 65–66) gives a list of some fifty clans grouped in twelve phratries for all the Hopi villages. The phratry system appears to be an old and well-established practice among the Hopi. Eggan (1950: 78–79) reports:

> The basic phratry pattern is more clearly delimited for the Hopi than are the constituent clan patterns. . . . It is evident that the phratry grouping has exerted an enormous stabilizing influence in Hopi society. Individual clans are subject to extinction from failure of the line or lines of women. This can happen rather rapidly, as the data for the last three generations indicate, particularly where the average population per clan group is small. The Hopi villages have been in existence since before 1540, the Oraibi at least probably

before 1200. With our present knowledge of the mechanisms for clan change, the basic pattern can only be due to the importance and conservatism of the phratry pattern, unless we are willing to assume that the clan-phratry pattern is recent among the Hopi. This is denied by the central importance of the clan and the uniqueness of the phratry pattern for the Hopi. . . .

Although there are seven Hano clans—Bear, Fir, Corn, Tobacco, Earth, Cloud, and Cottonwood—only two, Bear and Fir, are grouped together. This linkage seems identical with the phratry groupings of the Hopi and fits Titiev's definition of the Hopi phratry (Titiev 1944:58):

> . . . a nameless division of kindred made up of two or more clans which share certain privileges, mainly ceremonial, in common. The outstanding feature of the phratry is that it delimits the greatest extension of kinship terms based on a given relationship, and that it marks the largest exogamic unit recognized by the Hopi . . ."

All informants agree that this linkage occurred as recently as fifty or sixty years ago. The reason for merging is familiar Hopi theorizing. According to some informants, the two clans combined because in a migration legend the Fir clan is mentioned as a "pathmaker" for the Bear clan. Members of the clan assert that partnership in the past legitimatizes the linkage. Other informants report that the Fir clan was taken as a partner by the Bear clan when the Sun clan became extinct about fifty years ago. The Sun clan, along with Bear, Corn and Tobacco clans, made up the membership of Court Kiva (see Kiva Organization, Chapter 5). According to these informants, the extinction of the Sun clan disturbed the proper performance of certain ceremonies and another clan was needed to take its place. The Fir clan was therefore brought in to fill the vacancy. Kinship terms are extended to both clans, and marriages between members of the two clans are forbidden.

Members of the Fir and Cottonwood clans also consider themselves related to one another because "Fir and Cottonwood clans are both 'wood' or 'timber' clans." This grouping appears to be based on a familiar Hopi concept that "like" objects or "like" aspects of nature "belong together." On the same basis the Tewa Cottonwood clan is equated with the Hopi Kachina clan because Kachina dolls are made from cottonwood." There are no shared privileges, ceremonial or otherwise, between Fir, Cottonwood, or Hopi Kachina clans; nor are kinship terms and behavior extended; neither is marriage restricted. My own belief is that this grouping represents the initial stages of a phratral linkage which may eventually reach the full status of a Hopi phratry. Bear and Fir are the only Tewa clans linked in the Hopi fashion at present, that is, by (1) the sharing of certain ceremonial privileges; (2) extension of kinship terms, and, at least among some members, shared behavioral patterns; and (3) restriction of marriage between members of the two clans.

In good Hopi manner, members of the Bear and Fir clans now claim relationship to a host of clans present among the Hopi and other tribes. They rationalize the relationship not only on the basis that "like objects" or "like" aspects of nature belong together, but on the following principle. Hopi clans are considered to be partners "if they have shared mutual experiences during the mythical wanderings following the emergence." Thus, for example, Hopi Parrot and Crow clans are equated because of the following migration legend:

When the Parrot people stopped for the night they perched their guide, parrot, on the branch of a tree. On one occasion they built a fire underneath the branch of the tree where the parrot had been placed. They forgot about the bird until they were about to move again and when they looked up on the branch, they saw there a bird that looked like a crow (the pitch smoke of the fire had turned the parrot black). Some of the people said: "It is a crow, and we will take the name Crow for our people and descendants." That is why some people are Parrot clan and some Crow clan, but they are one people for they traveled together and did everything as a group.

On the basis of such theories the Hano Fir and Bear clan members claim relationship to members of the Hopi Bear, Bear's Eyeball, Bear's Bones, Carrying Strap, Spider, and Bluebird clans. In addition, they believe themselves related to strictly Hano "clans" which have developed, in name at least, independently of the Hopi: Mexican, Red Coral, Yellowwood, Aspen, Pine, Wood, and Stick. These are only alternate names for clans and do not have actual representation. They occur, however, as the names of actual clans among Navaho, New Mexico Pueblo, and other tribes and are, therefore, convenient to use for associating such clans with Hano Bear and Fir clans.

The incipient linkage between the Cottonwood and Fir clans has not been carried out as far as that between the Bear and the Fir. The other four Hano clans—Tobacco, Corn, Earth, and Cloud—are not associated with other clans. These clans are present among the Hopi, or at least are recognized as "alternate" names in phratry groupings. Among the Hopi, for example, Corn clan is associated with Cloud, Fog, Snow, and Patki (Water House). When I asked if the Hano Corn clan was also similarly related, my informant, a Corn clan woman, replied that the Tewa were not Hopi and she could not believe that a Hopi clan, even though similar in name, could be related to a Tewa clan. With regard to the association of Fir and Bear clans with certain Hopi clans, she remarked that these people "were trying to deny their Tewa heritage and wanted to be like Hopi." Yet when this same woman was on a visit to Mishongnovi in the winter of 1951, she sought out Patki households. At that time she remarked: "These are our people; they treat us kindly when we visit them, and when they come to our village they stay in our houses."

The remarks of this woman indicate the ambivalent attitude toward the Hopi already noted in Chapter 3. It is my belief that the four Hano clans which at present are still retaining their distinctiveness will soon find a reason for merging among themselves and with other Hopi clans, and will thus form phratries in the Hopi manner. This prediction is made in the view of the precedent already set by Bear and Fir clans and because the trend in other areas of Hopi and Hano culture seems to point toward social and cultural integration on First Mesa.

Hano has two kivas: Court Kiva and Outside Kiva. The seven Tewa clans are divided into these two kivas. The following are Court Kiva clans: Bear, Fir, Corn, and Tobacco. The Outside Kiva clans are Earth, Cottonwood, and Cloud. Before the Fir clan merged with the Bear clan its members belonged to the Outside Kiva; thus, while representatives of the Sun clan still lived (the Sun clan was aligned with the clans of Court Kiva), the two Hano kivas were evenly balanced, each having four clans. Today, the Cloud clan is almost extinct, since it has only one old woman of about eighty and three men left in it. About 50 years ago a Hano Tewa Cloud woman married a Shongopovi man and moved with her family to his village. The Tewa village denounced her for this violation of matrilocal residence. Shongopovi people say that the family moved out because the Tewa people were "mean" to her for marrying a Hopi man. Although the Cloud clan is extinct at Hano, the clan is represented at Shongopovi by several female members of the clan. These women speak no Tewa but proudly assert that they are Tewa and not Shongopovi Hopi. The surviving members of the Cloud clan at Hano are important, however, since they control the *Shumakoli,* the only association at Hano having the curing of illness as its sole objective (see Ceremonial Associations, Chapter 5). The fate of the Shumakoli when the present members of the Hano Cloud clan pass away will be resolved in one of three ways (if past precedent is followed): (1) One of the Shongopovi women may come with her family to live at Hano and thus reseed the clan and take over the management of the association; (2) another Hano clan may take charge of the association; or (3) the sacred fetish and masks of the curing association may be buried and the association permitted to die. Another alternative that would be employed by the Hopi is that the association could go to the lineage head of the Cloud clan at Shongopovi. This is unlikely, for the Hano do not permit the borrowing of their associations and ceremonies by the Hopi.

The division of clans in terms of the two kivas suggests the New Mexico Tewa moiety system. Indeed, some Hano individuals use the New Mexico Tewa words for summer and winter to designate the Court Kiva and Outside Kiva groups, respectively. It is possible, of course, that this usage has been borrowed in recent years from the frequent visits of the New Mexico Tewa; however there are other aspects of Hano social organization which seem to reveal a vestigial moiety organization. These aspects are most pronounced in ceremonial life and are therefore reserved for discussion in Chapter 5 under "Ceremonial Organization."

Hopi concepts of clan migrations and relative position of clans in terms of status are also beginning to influence the Hano Tewa. The migration legends of the Hopi follow a characteristic pattern (see Eggan 1950: 79). After the various Hopi clans emerged from the Underworld, they set out in various directions and ultimately arrived at one or another of the Hopi villages. When a clan arrived in a Hopi village, it secured land from the clan or clans that had preceded it. The newcomers were given the land in exchange for their performing a ceremony or providing protection from marauding enemies. The priority of arrival of clans at Hopi was thus very important in terms of prestige and status because, among other things, it determined land rights. The late arrivals were as a consequence relegated to more exposed sites in the villages and given poorer farm land. In terms of status these late arrivals occupied the lowest positions. Hopi logic is not consistent, however; it appears that certain clans, though arriving late, have elevated themselves to higher positions. Such changes appear to have taken place under certain fortuitous circumstances, perhaps with the rise of unusually capable leaders in a low-ranking clan or through the phratry pattern in which a late-arriving clan might be incorporated into a league with important clans. Eggan suggests that Hopi clan migration legends have been altered through the years to correlate *order* of arrival at Hopi with the ceremonial precedence of clans at any given time (Eggan 1950: 79).

Hano clans have developed migration legends similar to the Hopi, but with certain important differences. The Tewa of Hano believe that the migration took place in two groups, the clans of the Court Kiva coming first and those of the Outside Kiva following later. This pattern differs from that of the Hopi, who conceive of the individual clans as coming to Hopi separately.

In terms of status the Court Kiva clans claim that since they were the first to arrive on First Mesa, their position at Hano is similar to that of the original Snake and Bear clans at Walpi, whose leaders, according to tradition, asked the Tewa to come to Hopi. The role of the Court Kiva clans is sacred; they must pray and mediate for the welfare of all Tewa individuals. Among the Hopi, those clans believed to have arrived first are accorded sacred functions and carry the highest rank. In recent years, under the influence of increasing diffusion of Hopi concepts, the Court Kiva clans have begun to set themselves apart as the clans with the highest status. The fact that the Bear clan was once important at Walpi (the clan is now extinct, the Horn or Flute clan has assumed its duties and status); that the Bear clan is still important in other major Hopi villages; and that the Bear clan is one of the clans of the Court Kiva group has undoubtedly strengthened this rationalization. At present, as among other major Hopi villages, the chief of Hano comes from the Bear clan.

The following statement by a Bear clansman presents the situation as viewed by the court Kiva clans:

> Our group left *Tsawadeh* ahead of the other clans. When our clans arrived at Hopi they secured a village site and farm lands and then sent for the other clans. Because our duties are sacred, we need a warrior group to defend us. Fighting an enemy must always be done with a great deal of prayer and meditation. This is as important as the actual fighting; unless our warriors are helped by war magic they will not succeed. Sometimes our magic alone is sufficient to win a victory and we do not need to sacrifice lives.
>
> The Outside Kiva clans are subject to our dictates in all important matters. In anything that pertains to the welfare of the village these clans must meet with us before they act. Their duties are concerned primarily with outside matters [secular], whereas ours pertain to religion.

The Outside Kiva clans accept the Bear clan head as the Village Chief and also the notion that the court Kiva group of clans should devote themselves to prayer and meditation. However, they emphatically deny that they were late arrivals on First Mesa. Indeed, they report that as warriors they preceded the main migration of the entire group, clearing a path and making safe the journey. They also refuse to accept the idea that clans whose functions are devoted primarily to prayer and meditation should be regarded as "better" than other clans. The report of a Cottonwood clansman express this point of view:

> When our clans [Outside Kiva clans]left our home in the east they came directly to Hopi. This was in terms of an agreement made before the migration. Our clans were to secure a village site and farm lands and then send for the other clans. At Hopi our clans fought the enemy and then sent for the Court Kiva clans when the country had been made safe for habitation. These clans brought our sacred objects and our ceremonies, and once more we began to live as one people. There are no differences between us—we have different duties but we are the same people. We need each other to make a strong pueblo and to be effective as "protectors" of First Mesa.

It is difficult, perhaps impossible, to verify Hano—or Hopi—legends. Changes appear to be going on constantly to validate statuses, functions, or particular ceremonies. In the context in which the legends have been considered here, however, they are useful because they indicate quite clearly that the Hano are beginning to pattern their clan legends along Hopi lines.

The Kinship System

THE NATURE OF THE TERMINOLOGY Tewa kinship terms are mostly descriptive designations, that is, almost every kinship term consists of more than one word. Hopi kinship terms, on the other hand are classificatory, a single term being applied to more than one type of relationship. Only one term, the designation for older sister, *kakah*, appears to have been borrowed from the Hopi; all other terms are native Tewa and are either identical or cognate with those used among the New Mexico Tewa. It is interesting that even in kinship the purest tendencies of the Tewa with respect to their language have been exercised. As we have noted elsewhere, the vocabulary of the Tewa is free of Hopi words with the exception of this kin term and another, the male word for "thank you." Tewa girls and women use the native Tewa word for "thank you."

Like the New Mexico Tewa, siblings and mother's sisters are distinguished on the basis of seniority and the junior reciprocal is used extensively. In spite of these similarities to the New Mexico Tewa kinship system, Hano kinship structure differs hardly at all from the Hopi. The system, like that of the Hopi, is organized on a lineage principle, quite different from the bilateral generational type of the New Mexico Tewa (*cf.* Harrington 1912: 472–498; Dozier 1955: 242–257). Thus, the Hano Tewa kinship system seems to have been reorganized along the Hopi pattern without the terms themselves being greatly modified (see Eggan 1950: 141–144; Dozier 1954: 305–310).

KINSHIP BEHAVIOR The Tewa of Hano, like their Hopi neighbors, have most intensive relations with three lineages: the mother's, the father's, and the mother's father's matrilineal lineages (*cf.* Eggan 1950: 19–26, 141–144). Women occupy a central position in the kinship system, while men are marginal. Marriage is prohibted with anyone in the three lineages. This fact plus the custom of matrilocal residence take men away from their lineal relatives upon marriage. A married man's loyalties and responsibilities are then divided between his new household and his natal one. He assumes economic and affectional bonds in the household he enters through marriage, yet custom demands that he retain his loyalties and ceremonial duties to his lineal relatives. A Tewa man married to a Tewa woman experiences little conflict, since Hano as a village has greater unity, both social and cultural, than a Hopi village. The important cementing force at Hano is *being Tewa* and this fact tends to override other loyalties and commitments. Divided loyalties and responsibilities do arise in men married to Hopi women, however, and undoubtedly these factors have prevented large scale intermarriages with the Hopi in the past and have largely restricted Hopi-Tewa marriages in recent years to the three villages on First Mesa. A man may continue to interact frequently with Hano members if he lives at Sichomovi or Walpi, but such interaction is highly restricted if he is married into one of the more distant Hopi villages. The effect of Hopi-Tewa marriages has been a unification of the three villages on First Mesa and a greater sense of community organization. Lineal loyalties and responsibilities do not therefore result in the constant disruption of village integration so characteristic of other Hopi villages (*cf.* Eggan 1950: 118–119; Titiev 1944: 69). See Chapter 7 for a more detailed discussion of Hano, Hopi, and First Mesa integration.

In the following section, kinship behavior will be discussed in terms of the three lineages given prominence in the Hano kinship system.

MOTHER'S LINEAGE   Terminological differentiation is most complex and the relations most intense and intimate within the mother's lineage. Duties and responsibilities are also more specifically structured among these relatives. For a man these responsibilities are primarily ceremonial, especially once he has left his natal household and assumed economic duties in his wife's household. A woman's concern for her lineage is both economic and ceremonial, since she remains her entire life in her natal household and in constant association with her matrilineal relatives.

A younger sibling is called *tiye;* an older brother, *pipi,* and an older sister, *kakah.* Sex distinctions are made for older siblings but not for younger ones. It is interesting, however, that girls and women tend to refer to a brother as *pipi,* older brother, even though he may be younger than the speaker. Similarly, brothers generally refer to their sisters as *tiye,* younger sibling, regardless of age. The consideration of brothers as seniors and sisters as juniors and generally the importance given to seniority probably reflect a retention of New Mexico Tewa kinship usage. Among the latter, considerable emphasis is given to relative age, and male dominance is evident in certain patterns, such as the greater importance of the father in the household and male ownership of houses and land. The special recognition of seniority and male dominance in either terminology or behavior is not characteristic of the Hopi kinship system.

Before marriage brothers work together in common tasks, and cooperation in ceremonial activities continues after marriage even when brothers reside in separate households. A younger brother defers to an older one and the latter has the right to order, chastise, and demand obedience from a younger brother.

This is a privilege that is often exercised, and the younger brother obeys and listens attentively to an older brother's remonstrations. The older brother is also conceived of as the guardian of his younger siblings and is supposed to watch that they do not get injured or fall into mischief. When a younger sibling is hurt or gets into trouble, it is often said that it happened because the older brother was not attentive. If the discrepancy in age between a younger and an older brother is very great, the older brother may, in fact, take a position almost like that of mother's brother (see below). This is particularly true in families where the mother's brother has married into a distant household and is not always available to exercise discipline and lineage duties.

The relation of sisters to one another is very intimate and lifelong. Sisters rear and care for their children in the same household and cooperate in all household tasks. An older sister may often assume an importance equal to that of the mother in the household, particularly if she is the oldest daughter in the household and the other children are considerably younger than she. There is in Hano a special term, *kakah,* to distinguish older sister from her younger siblings.

While the terminological usage implies a deference to males, the actual behavior between a brother and a sister does not reveal patterns of subordination and superordination. There is a great deal of cooperation and exchange of confidences between brother and sister. Even though a brother and a sister are eventually separated by marriage and subsequent residence in different households, contact is still maintained. A sister often advises a brother about making a proper marriage, and frequently has much to say about whom her brother should marry. Sisters aid in the preparation of food on ceremonial occasions in which their brothers participate.

The behavior of maternal parallel cousins toward each other is comparable to that between siblings. Relative age is important, behavior and terms being adjusted accordingly. The terms used for maternal cousins are those for mother's siblings and the junior reciprocals of these terms, which are formed by adding *e,* "child" to the term. Thus, mother's sister's son if older than a male or female speaker is called *meme,* mother's brother; if younger, he is called *meme-e,* mother's brother (diminutive) by a male speaker and *ko-o-, e,* mother's younger sister (diminutive) by a female speaker. Mother's sister's daughter if older than a male or female speaker is called *ko-o;* if younger, she is called *meme-e* by a male and *ko-o-e* by a female. In behavior greater respect and obedience is consistently accorded an older maternal parallel cousin. Since these relatives ordinarily live together or in close proximity, the relations are frequent, intimate, and marked with deep attachment. In recent years, modern conditions have tended to limit the interaction of siblings and maternal parallel cousins by the necessary divisions of the extended household, but these relatives still come together frequently at social and ceremonial functions.

The mother-son (*yiyah* and *e*) relationship is deep and enduring. Even after a son leaves home at marriage, he frequently returns for aid and advice. A mother may scold and admonish her son, but this is her right as a mother, and the son is not ordinarily much disturbed by her anger. Serious advice and admonition are usually referred to the mother's brother, the disciplinarian of the household. A mother has the primary decision in the selection of her son's "ceremonial father" and gives the man who is chosen food and gifts in recompense for his services. Behavior between the mother and daughter (*yiyah* and *e*) is marked by cooperative activities and duties. The mother trains the daughter in all domestic duties: grinding corn, cooking, taking care of babies, and the like. A mother and daughter constantly confide in one another. At least in the recent past, a daughter immediately informed her mother of her first menstruation; her mother then took her to the girl's father's sister's house, and she underwent the puberty ceremony there (see Life Cycle below). Important ritual knowledge pertaining to the clan is transmitted from mother to daughter. A daughter has the deepest affection for her mother and constantly aspires to be like her.

The relation between *kaye* (mother's older sister) and her younger sister's children, *kaye-e* is different from that between *ko-o* (mother's younger sister) and the latter's older sister's children. *Kaye* demands more aid and gives more orders to her younger sister's children. In return she receives strict obedience from them. A younger sister often sends her children to be admonished or instructed in certain domestic and ritual duties by her older sister. This is particularly true if both the mother's mother (*saya*) and *saya's* sister (also called *saya*) are absent. Relations between *kaye* and her younger sister's son, *kaye-e*, are marked by the same affection and gentleness. Contacts between these two relatives are less frequent because of the difference in sex and if her nephew is married, but the relations that exist are mutually affectionate.

The position of *kaye* is superseded only by *saya* (mother's mother) in the household. She has a great deal to say about both the store of foodstuffs and ritual matters. As *saya* becomes old and less able to perform her duties, *kaye* takes on more and more authority and upon the former's death takes over her position.

It is obvious that behavioral patterns within the household are to a large extent determined by relative age. If a mother's sister is much older than her nieces and nephews though younger than their mother, she is still likely to be shown the deference and respect due a female lineal relative of mother's generation. However, if the mother's sister is approximately the same age as her nephews and nieces, the relations among all these relatives would be identical with the behavior generally exhibited among siblings. Behavior is also conditioned by the kind of relations that exist between a parent and the relative under consideration. An older maternal aunt, for example, may joke with her younger sister and order her around, and thus influence the behavior of her own children toward this relative. I recall a demonstration of this pattern of behavior in the Hano home where I made my residence during the course of fieldwork. In addition to other members the household contained an older maternal aunt, two of her grown daughters, and her younger sister who was *ko-o* to her daughters. When I asked the oldest daughter to let me take a photograph of her teen-age daughter, Josie, in the "cart-wheel" hairdress worn by girls after puberty, she called her *ko-o* to dress Josie's hair. As *ko-o* worked, the daughters joked with her. They said *ko-o* was slow and that she ought to work faster. If *ko-o* pulled on Josie's hair too hard, they laughed, much to the annoyance of both *ko-o* and little Josie. *Ko-o* remonstrated with her older sister's daughters, telling them that they were just like the girls of the younger generation, ignorant of traditional tasks, even a simple one such as dressing a girl's hair.

One of the most important of Hano kinship relationships is that of a man to his sister's children. The mother's brother, *meme*, is chief disciplinarian to his sister's children and they both respect and obey him. Usually the sister's oldest brother takes the role, but in his absence a mother's younger brother may be called to perform the function of disciplining his sister's children. The mother's brother is generally feared by the children, and often the mere mention of his name, with a threat to call him if the children do not behave, is enough to make them conform. Mother's oldest brother (if mother's mother's brother is not alive) is frequently the ritual head of the clan. He and mother are responsible for clan rituals and often get together to discuss such affairs. As a son or daughter grows up, *meme* becomes more of a confidant and a source of information, while his disciplinary functions diminish. It is true that *meme* is sometimes called to settle marital quarrels and to warn a young man not to drink, but this is infrequent as adults are expected to behave properly and generally do so.

Mother's mother and mother's mother's sister are called *saya;* the reciprocal is *saya-e*, grandmother (diminutive). The behavior of *saya* toward her *saya-e* is more indulgent and kind than that of a mother toward her child. Since a grandmother ordinarily lives in the same household as her grandchildren, she has frequent contacts with them. She rarely scolds a grandchild but provides a great deal of affection. A grandmother tells her grandchild stories and legends and instills in the young child a pride in being Tewa. A *saya* is loved dearly. A child will often seek her out in order to divulge his troubles to her, and he is always assured of a sympathetic reception and kindly counsel. While *saya* is strong and active, she is the head of the household and in charge of all foodstuffs. She possesses essential ritual knowledge and must be consulted in all important matters regarding the household and clan.

The *saya* of the household in which I lived during the course of fieldwork fully met these requirements and performed her duties as a good grandmother. Her grandchildren respected, obeyed, and loved her. They sought her out to confide in her and to have her arbitrate quarrels between themselves and others. One of the girls slept with her every night on a sheepskin pelt. The two youngest children in the household, a boy of two and a girl of four, always took a position beside their grandmother when visitors came. If they were teased, they hid behind her or buried their faces in her lap while *saya* spoke softly to them and stroked their hair.

The Hano Tewa recognize two relatives above the grandparent generation: *pahpa*, mother's mother's mother, and her brother, *pepe*. These relatives are usually extremely old and often are blind. Inevitably, then, the duty of their great-grandchildren and great-grandnephews and nieces is to see that they are conducted about the village and guided into the houses of their relatives. A *pahpa* or *pepe* is kindly and indulgent to all, and is respected and treated affectionately by all members of the community.

There is a wide range of individuals to whom the key relative terms of mother's lineage are extended. Extension of these terms embraces the clan and, in certain cases, linked clans of the Hopi, the Navaho, and the New Mexico Pueblo Indians. These terms incorporate the important individuals of the lineage and thus extend to those individuals designated by the terms some of the same respect accorded to members of the lineage.

The term *kaye*, mother's older sister is a general term for all senior women of one's clan. Younger women are called by the junior reciprocal, *kaye-e*, mother's older sister (diminutive). Very old women are' called *saya*, mother's mother.

All older men of one's own clan are called *meme*, mother's brother; and its junior reciprocal *meme-e*, mother's brother (diminutive), is applied to all very young members of the clan.

The terms given above are applied to all equivalent Hopi, Navaho, and New Mexico Pueblo clans. The New Mexico Tewa, regardless of clan affiliation, are called by clan terms as if they were of the same clan. For showing respect to Rio Grande Tewa individuals, the senior terms are employed even though the person addressed may be considerably younger. Thus, when I brought a group of Hano Tewa to my home in Santa Clara Pueblo (New Mexico) during the course of fieldwork, the visitors all called my sister *kaye* although she was younger than most of the visitors. They also used the term *meme* for male adults obviously younger than themselves. Only for children were the junior reciprocals used. At Hano I was called *meme* by the very old as well as by the very young.

Men who marry women of one's lineage are called *soyingih* (bridegroom) and women marrying men of one's lineage are designated *sai* (bride). Again these terms are applied to all men and women married to equivalent Hopi, Navaho, and New Mexico Pueblo clans. Similarly these terms are extended to men and women of non-Tewa extraction married to New Mexico Tewa regardless of clan affiliation. At Hano, my wife, although a white woman, was called *sai* by all. The parents and relatives of a spouse are called collectively *ya-a*, in-laws. A wife's or husband's father is *ya-seno*, relative man; a wife's or husband's mother is *yakwiyoh*, relative woman. There are ritual gift exchanges between the families of a couple at marriage, but relations between in-laws is on a personal level rather than one specified by kinship.

FATHER'S LINEAGE   Relations with one's father's and one's mother's father's lineage are almost identical, although by virtue of residence, where one's father lives in the same household, opportunities for interaction with the father's matrilineal relatives are most frequent and most intense. The special relations specified in the kinship system between the father's sisters and one's natal household also bring these relatives into more intimate relationship. The term *tutun* (father's brother) or *tadah* (father) is extended to all male members of father's lineage regardless of generation. They, in return, refer to a brother's son or daughter as *tu-e*, father's brother (diminutive). These relations are free of directive or authority overtones; they are relations of companionship and genuine affection.

The most important relative in father's matrilineage is father himself. He is the only member of his lineage that is a part of one's household (unless two sisters marry two clan brothers). A Hano father is the most loved relative in the household. His behavior toward his children is in direct contrast to that of the general American and European father. He neither directs, scolds, nor punishes; these are mother's, mother's sister's, and mother's brother's prerogatives. The father and indeed all classificatory fathers are affectionate confidants and companions. In part the affectionate behavior of a father may be prompted by a desire to entrench himself in the household in which he is an outsider. A wife's and her children's loyalties are primarily with their own lineage and clan; conversely, a husband is committed to his own lineage and clan. Through the custom of matrilocal residence and duties to his wife and children, however, he has responsibilities for supporting the whole household (with the aid of unmarried men of his wife's household and the men married into it). These conflicting roles make his position insecure and the marriage bond rather unstable (about 20 percent of Hano marriages end in divorce). The affectionate tie between a father and his children helps cement his position in the household. Children, because of the warm regard they have for their father, will often arbitrate controversies and effect compromises between father and mother.

The children of classificatory fathers are called by sibling terms: *pipi* (older brother), *tiye* (younger sibling), and *kakah* (older sister). One's relations with these relatives are not intimate. Interaction is infrequent since they live in separate households.

Women of father's lineage are called *kiyu* (father's sister) regardless of generation; reciprocals are *e-sen* (man child) and *e-kwiyoh* (woman child). Father's sisters manifest a deep interest in their *e-sen* from the time of his birth (see Life Cycle below) and continue a warm relationship for life. Usually a father's sister takes upon herself to become the special guardian of one of her brother's sons. Other women of father's clan may select other sons of their clansbrother on whom to bestow special attention and affection. Such a father's clanswoman appears in her brother's house at crucial periods of her brother's son's life. If he has been injured or is ill, his *kiyu* will come immediately to console him. When the ogre Kachina come on the morning before Powamu (an annual ceremony), she is at her brother's house to "protect" her *e-sen* from the child's own clansfolk, who "pretend to give away the child" to these frightful-appearing Kachinas (see Social Control below). As the boy becomes older, *kiyu* "pretends to be jealous" of her *e-sen's* regard for his girl friends.

During a buffalo dance in January 1951 two girls and two boys danced in the middle of the village courtyard. A woman spectator suddenly ran out among the dancers, pushed out one of the girls, and took the girl's position. She danced spiritedly for about five minutes and then returned among the spectators. The onlookers roared with laughter at this performance, but the woman's expression was one of mock seriousness and anger. Another woman brandishing a rifle also ran to the dancers. She pointed the weapon at the feet of one of the girls and pretended to fire it.

One of the women of the household in which I lived explained that these women were the boy dancers' *kiyu* and that they were "publicly displaying their jealousy and anger for their *e-sen's* girl partners."

When a brother's son marries, his *kiyu*, with other women of her clan, protests the marriage by attacking the boy's mother and mother's sisters in mock play. Even after a brother's son is married, his *kiyu* visits him and teases his wife, "pretending to make love to him."

A *kiyu* is "proud" of her *e-sen's* participation in social and ceremonial dances and helps prepare food for him. In return, an *e-sen* performs various services for his *kiyu*. He may make furniture or repair household fixtures for her. One of the sons of my hosts, for example, made and installed window screens for his *kiyu*. Formerly an *e-sen* brought his *kiyu* meat from game that he had killed and salt from salt expeditions. Mutually the relations are informal, affectionate, and lifelong. In the presence of each other's spouses the two "pretend to be like lovers" and speak of their deep attachment for one another, "to make the husband or wife jealous" (see the relations between a man and the husbands of women of father's lineage below).

A father's sister's relations with her brother's daughter lacks the public display of mock behavior. She participates in the naming ceremony of her *e-kwiyoh* (woman child) and protects, aids, and provides affection at crucial periods in the girl's development. She guides her through the puberty ceremonies at the time of the girl's first menstruation. At this time the father's sister also puts up the girl's hair in "cart-wheels," the symbol signifying a girl's availability for courtship. As adults, the two visit one another frequently, confide in each other, and assist in household duties.

Father's mother is also called *kiyu*, but if she has cut the umbilical cord and conducted the naming ceremony, she is called *kuku*. The reciprocal is *ku-e*, umbilical-cord-cutter (diminutive). The relation between *kuku* and her grandchild is similar to that between *saya* and the latter's grandchild. If *kuku* is young, however, she may behave toward her grandchild very much as a *kiyu* does to her *e-sen* and *e-kwiyoh*. *Kuku* will protect and aid her grandchild during the child's growth and development. More frequently, however, the relation between *kuku* and her grandchild is kindly, indulgent, and affectionate.

The Hano Tewa select ceremonial sponsors for certain stages of the life cycle and for crises situations (see Life Cycle below). Four categories of ceremonial sponsors exist: (1) A ceremonial "father" is selected for a boy between the ages of eight and ten, and a ceremonial "mother" for a girl of similar age, when the boy or girl enters the Kachina cult. (2) A ceremonial "father" inducts a young man into the Winter Solstice ceremony when he is between twelve and sixteen years old. Women are not inducted into this ceremony, but at a comparable age they grind corn for four days and have their hair style changed to "cart-wheels" (see above). (3) A "doctor father" is selected for a man or boy who is very ill (a "doctor mother" for a woman or girl); he is supposed to cure the patient who is given to him in "adoption." (4) A ceremonial sponsor—a man for a boy and a woman for a girl—is selected for a young person about to become a member of a curing society.

The ceremonial sponsor must be from a clan other than that of the novice, but he may be of the novice's father's clan. The Hano Tewa believe that a novice becomes a member of his (or her) sponsor's clan. The relations between a novice and his ceremonial sponsor are, however, much more affectionate than that which exists between members of the same clan. These relations are indeed more like those between father and son or between father's sister and her brother's child. The term "father" is used for a male sponsor, but "mother" for a female sponsor; the reciprocal is simply *e*, "child." Thus, the father's lineage terms are not consistently applied, although the behavior shown by one toward the two sets of relatives is similar for other members of the sponsor's clan; the novice uses his own lineage terms.

Women married to men of father's lineage are referred to as *yiyah* (mother) but one has no special relations with them.

Men who marry women of father's lineage are treated as joking relatives. Such a husband is called *thete* (grandfather); the reciprocal is simply the diminutivized form *thete-e*. The term is the same used for men of mother's father's matrilineal lineage, but the behavior that exists toward the two sets of relatives is not at all comparable. The behavior toward the first set of relatives is a form of releasing aggression in a culturally approved fashion, whereas the second set are respect relatives. Sons and the husbands of father's clanswomen engage in a battle of verbal wit and may even scuffle around with each other. They constantly belittle one another. They invent uncomplimentary nicknames for each other and use them at social gatherings to provide humorous entertainment for all present. On one occasion I happened upon a spirited wrestling match between two men I knew intimately. Ordinarily, the Tewa (like the Hopi) do not fight one another, but these two actually seemed angry at each other, and they struggled earnestly for almost an hour. A group of onlookers gathered; from their laughter and comments I soon learned that these two men stood in the relationship of *thete* and *thete-'e*.

Relations between a woman and her father's clanswomen's husbands also involve joking and name-calling, but no physical contacts occur between them.

MOTHER'S FATHER'S MATRILINEAL LINEAGE   Mother's father's matrilineal relatives are called *thete* (grandfather) and *thete kwiyoh* (grandfather's woman) again regardless of generation. The behavior shown to these relatives and to those of one's father's lineal kinfolk is similar. Conceptually these relatives appear to be somehow equated. Behavior of *thete* toward his grandchildren is marked by kindness and deep affection. If a grandfather is still strong and vigorous, he may take his grandchild or grandnephew with him when he goes into the fields and there teach him the simple farming techniques of the Hopi and Tewa. He will also guide him in other tasks, patiently and affectionately watching to see that the boy does a good job. If the grandfather is Tewa, he will tell his grandchild all about the Tewa migration legend and the curse on the Hopi, and he will teach him Tewa songs. Very old Tewa are extremely proud of their Tewa heritage and try under all circumstances to develop such pride in younger children.

A middle-aged, acculturated Tewa man gave me the following account of his boyhood relations with his maternal grandfather:

Whenever I went to see *thete* he made me sit beside him and told me the Tewa migration legend which I had heard countless times from his lips. I knew the story so well that I could probably relate it better than he. *Thete* would start from the beginning, repeating all important events four times, as is the traditional pattern in all legends. His voice would become charged with emotion when he spoke of the injustices the Tewa suffered from the Hopi, and he always ended the legend by telling me that we Tewa must never forget this story, but must always tell it to our children as he had related it to me. I became so tired of the story that I would try to invent some excuse so that I would not have to listen to it again. Sometimes I went to sleep while he was telling the story, and then he would shake me gently and tell me that I must not sleep, that the story was very important, and that I must learn it well. Sometimes I became angry with *thete;* surely the Hopi were not as bad as he would have me believe. My own father is Hopi and I love my father dearly and all of my *kiyu* are wonderful to me. But my grandfather was old and I did not want to offend him by telling him these things or by going away without hearing the end of the story.

The paternal grandfather is also called *thete* (grandfather) and *thete kwiyoh* (grandfather's woman), which is also applied to father's father's sisters. The maternal grandfather normally lives in one's household and hence sees his daughter's children often and the latter also interact with his sisters frequently, hence the relations among these relatives is intimate. On the other hand, the paternal grandfather lives in a different household and his sisters still in another, hence interaction is infrequent in spite of the fact that the same terms are used for these relatives.

Life Cycle

An account of the development of an individual from birth to death will clarify the relations and behavior between the various relatives already discussed and give us a better understanding of how a Tewa becomes a participating member of his culture. After presentation of the life cycle, the significant aspects of the kinship system will be summarized and discussed.

The Hano Tewa have a rather elaborate ritual at birth that differs only in minor details from the Hopi. Parsons (1921: 98–104) gives a First Mesa Hopi account with references to Hano practices. During the course of my fieldwork a number of the children were born in the hospital at Keams Canyon, and the customary ritual was not, of course, carried out completely. Even in such cases, however, the naming ceremony is performed for the child as soon as it is returned to the village. Hano women usually try to have their babies in the village in the traditional manner, but in recent years a few women have been persuaded by government employees and white friends to go to the hospital. Since men are excluded, I was not able to attend any of the native birth rites but I obtained the following brief account from the senior woman of the household in which I resided. The account is similar to the one given by Parsons (1921:98–104) for First Mesa Hopi. My hostess reported:

If my daughter is going to have a baby she will have it in this house. I will call my sister and also my sister's older daughters who have already had children. We will darken the room by hanging blankets over the door and windows. Only women will be present, none of the men. If she has trouble having the child, we may call a "doctor" [a native medicine man] to help her. After the child is born I will call my *yakwiyoh*, my daughter's husband's mother, and she will cut the umbilical cord. *Yakwiyoh* [called *kuku* by the child after it is grown] cuts the cord with an arrow shaft if the baby is a boy and with a corn-gruel stirring rod if the baby is a girl. She then places fine ashes on the navel.

After the baby is born my daughter and her baby are cared for by her *yakwiyoh* [women of her husband's clan] for twenty days. They comb and bathe my daughter and make certain that she is kept warm all of the time. She is given hot corn-meal gruel and may drink only boiled juniper water; she cannot have pure water, meat, or salt. The baby is washed right after birth by *yakwiyoh* and sprinkled with fine ashes. This is repeated every four days for the twenty days that my daughter and her baby are in confinement in the darkened room. An ear of white corn is kept next to the baby all of the time "to guard the baby."

On the nineteenth day the women of my house and my sisters' houses [women of the extended household] prepare *piki* [paper-thin bread made from blue corn meal], corn pudding, stews, and other food. Before sunrise the next day all the women of my daughter's husband's clan come to the house. Each woman dips an ear of corn in a bowl of yucca suds and touches the head of the baby four times and then with a prayer gives it a name. The name is from her clan—something which describes her clan. If the baby's father is Tobacco clan, the baby may be named tobacco blossom; or maybe yellow leaf, describing the tobacco plant when it is ripe. As the sun comes up, *yakwiyoh* takes the baby outside and utters all the names that have been given to it. Out of the many names, the baby's mother and father will decide which is the prettiest and will call the baby by that name.

The infant is nursed by the mother and is cared for primarily by her, but soon he begins to become a real part of the extended household. His brothers and sisters and his mother's sisters and their children start playing an important role in his training. *Saya* mother's mother, is also frequently on the scene. For the first six or seven years of life socialization takes place almost entirely within the confines of the extended household. At the age of seven or eight, however, the child starts to go to school at the government day school at Polacca. This takes him out of the secure and familiar surroundings of the household for the first time.

The day school can be either a relatively easy adjustment for the child or a seriously disturbing one. Under a patient and indulgent teacher the transition may even be a pleasant one, opening new experiences and new horizons for the child. Unfortunately, such teachers are in the minority. Although a teacher may sincerely wish to adjust Hopi and Tewa children comfortably into an unfamiliar situation, the teacher's own value orientation is often completely different. The ordinary American teacher on an Indian reservation tries to instill in his pupils such American principles as saving, individual responsibility, competition, and a dozen others entirely alien to the Hopi or Tewa child. In the process, the child becomes confused, and disturbance to the child's personality structure may result. Not only do the goals of his teachers conflict with those of the child's traditional cultural values and training, but the child is suddenly confronted with a puzzling and bewildering maze of new technological equipment to which he must adjust: washbasins, toilets, pencils, papers, and a myriad other new things not present in his home environment.

Hano children are perhaps more fortunate in the school situation than Hopi children. The more aggressive characteristics of the Tewa generally and the fact that they are or have been in the recent past a minority group (with respect to the Hopi) have made them more receptive to American cultural values. Moreover, the necessity of having to learn a new language is not a strange phenomenon to a Hano child. Hano children have been in a bilingual situation for more than 250 years. A Tewa child learns the Hopi language almost simultaneously with Tewa. English is not an entirely unfamiliar language either. He has heard his parents, his brothers, and his sisters use it on various occasions. I have many times observed adult Tewa teaching young relatives English words and delighting in the successful attempts of the children in mastering a few words.

When not in school Hano children learn the more traditional aspects of their culture. A boy accompanies his father to the fields and slowly learns about farming through observation and by actually doing some of the work. A girl also learns household duties in the same way, from the women of the household.

Between eight and ten years of age both boys and girls are initiated into the Kachina cult. A ceremonial father is selected for the boy and a ceremonial mother for the girl. These sponsors are from a clan other than that of the child. The initiation rites are held four days before Powamu, a Hopi ceremony in which the Hano Tewa participate. Parents, ceremonial sponsors, and all the acquaintances of a child have dramatized and made these activities extremely important in his thinking. A child who is going to be initiated exhibits tremendous excitement long before the event takes place. An adult male Tewa reported his initiation experiences as follows:

We were told that the Kachina were beings from another world. There were some boys who said that they were not, but we could never be sure, and most of us believed what we were told. Our own parents and elders tried to make us believe that the Kachina were powerful beings, some good and some bad, and that they knew our innermost thoughts and actions. If they did not know about us through their own great power, then probably our own relatives told the Kachina about us. At any rate every time they visited us they seemed to know what we had thought and how we had acted.

As the time for our initiation came closer we became more and more frightened. The ogre Kachina, the Soyoku, came every year and threatened to carry us away; now we were told that we were going to face these awful creatures and many others. Though we were told not to be afraid, we could not help ourselves. If the Kachina are really supernaturals and powerful beings, we might have offended them by some thought or act and they might punish us. They might even take us with them as the Soyoku threatened to do every year.

Four days before Powamu our ceremonial fathers and our ceremonial mothers took us to Court Kiva. The girls were accompanied by their ceremonial mothers, and we boys by our ceremonial fathers. We stood outside the kiva, and then two whipper Kachina, looking very mean, came out of the kiva. Only a blanket covered the nakedness of the boys; as the Kachina drew near our ceremonial fathers removed the blankets. The girls were permitted to keep on their dresses, however. Our ceremonial parents urged us to offer sacred corn meal to the Kachina; as soon as we did so they whipped us with their yucca whips. I was hit so hard that I defecated and urinated and I could feel the welts forming on my back and I knew that I was bleeding too. He whipped me four times, but the last time he hit me on the leg instead, and as the whipper started to strike again, my ceremonial father pulled me back and he took the blow himself. "This is a good boy, my old man," he said to the Kachina. "You have hit him enough."

For many days my back hurt and I had to sleep on my side until the wounds healed.

After the whipping a small sacred feather was tied to our hair and we were told not to eat meat or salt. Four days later we went to see the Powamu ceremony in the kiva. As babies, our mother had taken us to see this event; but as soon as we began to talk, they stopped taking us. I could not remember what had happened on Powamu night and I was afraid that another frightening ordeal awaited us. Those of us who were whipped went with our ceremonial parents. In this dance we saw that the Kachina were really our own fathers, uncles, and brothers. This made me feel strange. I felt somehow that all my relatives were responsible for the whipping we had received. My ceremonial father was kind and gentle during this time and I felt very warm toward him, but I also wondered if he was to blame for our treatment. I felt deceived and ill-treated.

After the Powamu ceremony my head was washed and I received a new name. At this time, too, the small feather was removed from my hair and the food restrictions were lifted.

The traumatic experiences of the Kachina initiation are deeply embedded in the memory of all Hano Tewa. Yet most of them felt that the whippings were not harmful but on the contrary were good for the child. Although no relative will lay a hand on a child, the whippings of the Kachina are considered to have a favorable effect on the subsequent behavior of the individual. There were similar expressions of opinion among those with whom I discussed the subject. "Hopi and Tewa children are well-behaved because they are disciplined early in life." "A human being needs to be broken, like a horse, before he can become a well-behaved individual." Many of the older Tewa ascribe the "meanness" of school trained boys and girls to the fact that they have not gone through this experience. For the same reason some parents defend the old military type of government boarding school where children were heavily disciplined. Missionary boarding schools, which follow a rather strict regime, are also preferred by some to the more informal and relaxed modern government or public boarding schools.

Tewa males are qualified to impersonate Kachina characters after the first initiation and soon assume such roles. Girls take on a more active part in household duties after this event, and boys acquire more responsibilities and heavier tasks in farming and ranching activities. Schooling provided by the day school ends about the time a boy or girl has reached the age of fourteen or fifteen. At this time another important event awaits them. For the boy the event is membership in the Hano Winter Solstice Association, and the initiation is generally simple but of great significance. After this event a boy is considered a man and is eligible for active membership in other Hano religious associations. A few Tewa men (and fewer women) also join the tribal associations of the Hopi after gaining membership in the Hano Winter Solstice Association (see Chapter 5).

Membership in the Winter Solstice Association requires the selection of another ceremonial father, generally not the same as the previous one. The ceremonial father must be a man who is not of the boy's clan, but a man whose clan belongs to the same kiva group with which the boy's clan is affiliated (see above, Lineage and Clan).

For four days before the Winter Solstice ceremony in December, the boy abstains from meat and salt. He is constantly in the care of his ceremonial father during this time; he eats his meals at the man's home and also sleeps there. Finally, on the night of the fourth day he accompanies his ceremonial father to the kiva. If his clan is affiliated with Court Kiva, he goes into that one; if he belongs to the Outside Kiva, he enters that one. The Winter Solstice ceremony is an all-night affair. To members the event is announced sixteen days before, and prayer sticks are made by the members who are in retreat there. The final night of the ceremony consists of the singing of songs and the telling of migration legends and past experiences of the Tewa by the chief of the group of clans that belong to that kiva. The novitiates sit next to their ceremonial fathers and listen attentively in order to learn the songs, legends, and stories told that night. The retreat terminates just before daybreak when the manufactured prayer sticks are taken out and deposited in the various shrines and springs surrounding Hano. The ceremony is strictly a Hano one; no Hopi are permitted to attend.

The second important event in a girl's life occurs at the time of her first menstruation. A woman keeps close watch over her daughter and instructs her to report all her physiological symptoms. When a mother is informed by her daughter that her menstrual period has begun, she brings one of her husband's sisters, the girl's *kiyu*. This woman then takes charge of the girl. She is secluded in the grinding room of *Kiyu's* house and grinds corn for four days. During this time she abstains from meat and salt and must use a scratching stick to scratch herself. In her chores she is assisted by her *Kiyu*, one of whom is constantly with her. There is a general atmosphere of good natured humor, and the conversation is informal and lively. At the end of the four days one of the *Kiyu* washes the girl's hair and fixes it in the "cart-wheel" fashion of the Hopi. The girl is also given a new name at this time.

The foregoing sketch of a girl's puberty rite was given as a definite "ideal." My Tewa informants reported that this custom was no longer consistently observed. My Hano hostess told me that her own daughter had at first objected to going through the ceremony, but had been persuaded to observe the ritual. The first initiation—the Kachina initiation—is in fact observed religiously. My hostess remarked:

> We still have control of our children when they are young, but schools and white contacts make them so independent that by the time they are twelve or fourteen they are difficult to manage. They get mad when we tell them to go through the rites. School girls hate to grind corn, and we old women have to do it all the time. The boys are better; they do not mind going to the kiva and performing their duties like their uncles and ceremonial fathers tell them to do.

Boys do not mind joining the Winter Solstice Association, actually membership into either the Outside Kiva or Court Kiva. The initiation rites are not difficult and involved, but on the contrary are even pleasurable. The twenty-six-year-old youth in the household in which I resided told me that "it was fun to attend the Winter Solstice ceremony and listen to the old Hano songs and to hear the old men tell of the experiences of our forefathers."

After a boy's initiation into the Winter Solstice Association and a girl's participation in the puberty ceremony, they are theoretically ready for marriage. Hano marriages, however, do not ordinarily take place until a youth is between twenty and twenty-five and a girl between eighteen and twenty-two. Courtship is, like that of the Hopi, strictly in the hands of the two persons concerned (cf. Eggan 1950: 54). Marriage restrictions are based on kinship and, except for the one prohibiting marriage within one's own clan, are not generally observed at present. Marriage between a couple belonging to the same clan is strictly prohibited, however, and there was not a single violation of this rule in the marriages recorded at the time of fieldwork. Although marriage is an individual matter, opinions of a person's siblings and father's sisters have an important influence in his choice of a mate.

Teen-age boys and girls have a maximum opportunity to see each other. Parents or other members of the household do not keep a check on the activities of grown children. Boys and girls meet under the protecting eaves of the cliffs, around the trading post, or in the proximity of the day school during the evenings. Although, according to reports, formerly a boy stole in late at night to a girl where she slept in her house, this is no longer a customary pattern of courtship. Premarital sexual relations are the rule, and the birth of children before marriage is common. Generally, however, a girl marries the father of her child and tries to do so before her child is born.

Marriage customs are similar to those of the Hopi as reported in the existing literature (cf. Titiev 1944: 30–43; Eggan 1950: 53–57). Marriages usually take place in January and August. According to Hano belief, marriages should not be contracted in the Kachina season, from February through July. January and August are considered the months for gaiety, the time when social dances and other happy events take place.

When a couple has decided to marry, the girl presents the boy's mother with piki (maize bread) and receives meat in exchange. Then follows a period of several weeks in which the women of the girl's household grind corn. When a large amount of corn has been ground, the girl is dressed in traditional Tewa dress and her hair is fixed in "cart-wheels." The girl is then taken to the house of the boy by her maternal and paternal kinswomen. The girl grinds corn in the boy's house for three days, and early on the fourth morning her hair is washed by the boy's maternal kinswomen.

While the girl is in her prospective husband's household, the boy's father's clanswomen may "object" to the marriage. These women descend on the boy's house and bedaub his mother and sisters with mud for letting their *e-sen* get away from them. They speak slightingly of the bride, saying that she does not deserve so fine a husband, and point out her flaws in personality and appearance. This is all done, however, in a spirit of fun, and any damage is later paid for.

In the meantime, the boy's male relatives on both his father's and his mother's side prepare the girl's wedding garments; these consist of belt, robe, dress, and moccasins. When the garments are completed, the girl dons the new outfit and her hair is dressed in the style of a Hano married woman. This hair style differs from that of the Hopi; it is similar to that of the New Mexico Tewa in that the sides are clipped. Hopi married women part the hair and with a string twist the locks on either side of the face.

The bride and bridegroom are then taken by his mother to her (the mother's) house. Early the next morning the boy's head is washed by the girl's clanswomen. The corn meal ground in the preceding weeks by the girl's relatives is then taken to the boy's household "as payment for depriving the family of a worker."

In addition to ground meal, enormous amounts of other food are taken to the boy's house. In this practice, Hano appears to differ from the Hopi generally. A Hopi teacher at Shongopovi told me that none of the Hopi villages matched the Tewa community in the amounts of food brought. Indeed, there is an effort on the part of the girl's relatives to bring more food and to display it more elaborately in front of the bridegroom's mother's home than was done for any previous marriage. In this respect there is a real spirit of competition.

Marriages in the traditional manner, as described above, are still popular. Couples who are married in a church or by a justice of the peace will return to have an "Indian wedding" as soon as possible. Sometimes the traditional wedding is performed first, and then the couple goes through a civil or church ceremony.

Residence is matrilocal, despite the fact that a couple may live separately in a part of the girl's mother's house or may even build a new home in another part of the village or at Polacca. The term "matrilocal residence" is justified because the new residence is built primarily with the help of the girl's extended family and on her clan lands. After the couple has started housekeeping, interaction is primarily with the wife's relatives as illustrated in the discussion of the household.

As time passes, a man becomes more and more entrenched in his new household. He forms ties that bind him ever more strongly to the relatives of his wife. The longer the two remain together, the more secure the marriage tie becomes. We have already noted that children are important in keeping a couple together; perhaps equally as important are the well-working relationships a man establishes with his wife's relatives.

A Tewa husband and wife may be very devoted to each other but they never openly demonstrate their affection. Husbands and wives are often together, however; they go to the spring, to the corrals, or to the trading posts together. A husband usually walks two or three paces in front while his wife trudges behind. This is the Hopi and Tewa manner for a husband and wife to walk, however, and is not indicative of subordinate or superordinate relationship. Hano marriages appear to be set in firmer foundations than Hopi ones, at least when compared with marriage and divorce figures obtained for the Hopi community of Oraibi. The divorce rate for Oraibi is almost 40 percent (see Titiev 1944: 34–35). The Hano Tewa figure is about half the Oraibi rate; of 144 married Tewa in 1950–1951, only 23 had been divorced previously.

The Hano Tewa believe that sickness is caused by bad thoughts, quarreling, witchcraft, and the breech of taboo. Hano ceremonialism and the admonitions of the Village Chief, Outside Chief, clan chiefs, association chiefs, and maternal uncles constantly emphasize the necessity of purging oneself and the community of these disease-producing agents. Prayer sticks and prayer feathers made by members of a ceremonial association during its retreat or by a group preparing to put on a social dance are placed in the shrines in order to induce the gods to keep the community healthy and the environment appeased (that is, to prevent inclement weather and to provide abundant moisture for crops). Social dances and repeat performances of Kachina dances are requested by individuals for advancing personal, family, and community well-being (see Chapter 5 for distinction between social and ceremonial rites). Public appearance of social dancers, ceremonial association members, and Kachina performers are made beautiful and exacting in order to impress the supernaturals and thus ensure for the people the blessings of good health and a bountiful harvest. The people must "have good thoughts and not be angry at anyone, nor quarrel with one another." This is important at all times, but it is vital during important ceremonials: "Some people are witches" and they are trying to cause illness and the failure of crops; it is therefore important to counteract these evil influences by concentrating on the proper performances of ceremonials. Ceremonial leaders warn initiates and participants in the various ceremonies to observe the exacting ritual carefully and to guard against the breaking of food restrictions and sexual-continence regulations. The Tewa believe that only by strict observance of all these rules can the community be assured of a healthy existence.

The Tewa of Hano thus attempt to appease the environment and ward off illness by ceremonial activity and through the constant vigilance and admonitions of ceremonial leaders. In addition, on an individual level, a person who has a serious ailment may be dedicated to a "doctor father" or may engage the services of a medicine man. An individual may also help cure an illness or injury by sprinkling sacred meal on the Kachina dancers in a kiva or courtyard performance. Another method, believed to be similarly efficacious, is to submit voluntarily to a whipping by the Whipper Kachina during the Kachina initiation rites in February. Injuries and the common communicable diseases are now referred to Public Health nurses and dotors, but lingering illnesses such as rheumatism and similar maladies are treated by medicine men.

The failure of the community to observe the precautions discussed above, or to prevent sickness by prescribed methods, results in drought, disease, and death. Death in old age is considered natural, but death in the prime of life is always attributed to one of the disease-producing agents already noted. No formal ceremonial wailing is practiced; the body is interred as quickly as possible. A woman is buried in her wedding outfit; a man is wrapped in a blanket. Burial grounds are at the foot of the mesa on the southeast side. After burial, the relatives of the deceased avoid mentioning his name and refrain from commenting about the circumstances surrounding his death.

Key Features of the Kinship System and Life Cycle

It is clear from the foregoing analysis that lineal relatives are emphasized in the kinship system and the life cycle. The primary relationships involving authority and control are centered in the matrilineal, matrilocal household. The women of one's lineage have the duty and responsibility of running the household; the mother's brother is charged with primary disciplinary powers. The father and his sisters and brothers, on the other hand, have a very different relationship to a person. Except for the father, these kin live in a different household. They have no authority in managing one's household or in disciplining him; they provide aid and affection.

The mother's father's matrilineal relatives keep alive the cultural heritage, teaching a child songs and telling him stories and legends. Tewa grandfathers try to instill in their Tewa grandchildren pride in being Tewa and insist that the child should always remember his distinct heritage. These relationships are unstructured; no specified duties or relationships like those which characterize relations with one's own or with one's father's matrilineal relatives.

Another set of relatives provides an interesting function in the socialization of the individual. These are the husbands of father's sisters, who tease and even engage in physical fights with a boy or man. The victim is permitted to retaliate and does so with increasing vigor and frequency as he gets older. A girl or woman may also engage in loud talk, "pretending to be angry" with her father's sisters' husbands, but does not strike them.

Thus we see that along with the emphasis of the matrilineal household and lineage the Tewa kinship system also channelizes behavior in an interesting manner among four sets of relatives. Authority and control is the prerogative of one's mother and her sisters and brothers; affection, aid, and comfort during crises periods of individual's growth is provided primarily by the father and his brothers and sisters; continuance of traditional lore is furthered by the mother's father's lineal relatives; and the release of aggression is provided in a culturally approved fashion by father's sisters' husbands. For women the customs prevalent at the time of marriage, when the bridegroom's father's clanswomen descend on his (the father's) house and vigorously protest the marriage, provide another social release of aggression.

The differences in the kinship system of the Hopi and the Hano Tewa are worth repeating. Along with the retention of their Tewa language, the Hano Tewa have also retained kinship terms that are the same or obviously cognate with New Mexico Tewa terms. The Tewa husband-wife bond appears to be more enduring. Among the Tewa the mother's sisters are differentiated terminologically as older and younger, and differential treatment is accorded them, a distinction not made by the Hopi. Similarly, older siblings are accorded greater respect and obedience by the Hano Tewa. These differences appear to be vestigial holdovers from the bilateral, generational kinship system of the New Mexico Tewa.

Changes in the kinship system as a result of modern conditions are evident primarily in the extended household. Interaction brought about by wage work and livestock activities is breaking up the household unit and dispersing its members in terms of nuclear family groups. However, since social and ceremonial functions bring about frequent resumptions of extended-household living, the integrity of the household unit still has great significance to the Tewa. The deep satisfactions derived from social interaction and ceremonies are important in this respect, and so too is the automobile, which makes it possible for members of the extended household to interact frequently.

Analysis of the life cycle has also revealed another area in which modern pressures have brought changes. Tewa girls are resisting traditional patterns of work, particularly those connected with puberty rites. Girls are doing their hair in modern style and are objecting to the tedious roles of grinding corn. The number of girls who go through the puberty ceremonies is admittedly decreasing. Changes in the roles of men with respect to the life cycle are not pronounced. We shall see, however, that there are marked changes in the ceremonial system, an area of Tewa culture in which men have a prominent role. The other significant events in a person's life—birth, marriage, and death practices—appear to be less affected by modern pressures.

In spite of changes and increasing pressures from the outside world, the Tewa kinship system is still remarkably strong and functional, at the present time.

Social Control

Social control is vested in two agencies, the matrilineal extended family and the village as a whole. Within the extended household, the mother's brother, or in his absence, any adult male of the household or clan, is responsible for the maintenance of order and the discipline of younger members. The details of this process have been discussed in the section on kinship behavior. In the village social control is exerted through gossip, public ridicule, social ostracism, and, at least in the past, by the charge of witchcraft. In addition, the Village

Chief, the Outside Kiva Chief, the War Chief, and the Kachina, particularly the Soyoku (Hopi and Hano bogeyman) have social control functions.

Gossip is the most common form of social control on the village level. During the fieldwork period, Tewa gossip denounced a man who suddenly began to take an active part in the Hopi Powamu Association. Ordinarily Tewa do not join Hopi associations, but this man through his Hopi father and Hopi ceremonial father participated enthusiastically in the association's activities. There were many phrasings of disapproval: "We have our own ceremonies; they should not be mixed with the Hopi." "If he wants to be a Hopi he should not be permitted in our kivas." "Don't let him take part in the Winter Solstice cere- mony next December." Eventually gossip reaches its victim and since a Tewa values Hano approval, he will ordinarily conform. Hopi criticism is often ig- nored, but disapproving gossip from one's community is taken seriously.

Public ridicule of a person who behaved improperly was formerly the special prerogative of the Koyala, or clown society. At present the society is ex- tinct, but volunteer or appointed clowns often ridicule individuals during cer- tain plaza dances. According to informants, the antics of the clowns today are mild, and it is said "they are afraid to make fun of town members." Instead, Navaho and whites become the subjects of ridicule.

On the occasion of a Kachina dance at Hano, I was once the target of the Koyala's antics. Tewa friends had told me many times that I smoked too much, and apparently on this occasion the Koyala had been instructed "to teach me a lesson." I was with friends, sitting with my back against the wall of a house and gingerly puffing on a cigarette. The clowns climbed a house next to the one I was sitting by and then crossed over to the roof of the house directly above me. I was conscious of the presence of the clowns, but for the moment the Kachina dance in the middle of the plaza occupied my attention. Then suddenly I heard the clowns yelling, "Fire! Fire!" I turned to look up and caught a buck- etful of water in my face. I was thoroughly drenched. The spectators laughed heartily at my discomfiture, and my hostess laughingly remarked: "Now maybe you will not smoke so much!"

Only one case of social ostracism and exile was related to me, but I was told that there were others in the past. This case involved the prominent and prosperous Tom Polacca whose name identifies the budding community at the foot of First Mesa. During the greater part of his life Polacca was highly re- spected and esteemed, but in later years he lost the good will of his community. Before his death Polacca departed from the traditional pattern of life and was converted to Mormonism. The ire of Hano was aroused, however, when the Tewa learned that Polacca had sold his house and land below the mesa to the Baptist Mission—land to which he had only use right. Polacca and his family were exiled to Sand Dunes, five miles from First Mesa and he was forever pro- hibited from participating and viewing Tewa ceremonies.

The Tewa are reticent to discuss witchcraft. I knew of no one who was accused or suspected of witchcraft. The following general statement was obtained from a highly acculturated Tewa man:

People are never told that they are witches to their face. But, for example, if members of a family do not participate in ceremonies or help in the cooperative enterprises of the pueblo, they are "talked about." If anything goes wrong, if many people get sick, or if it does not rain, then some people may say: "It is because that family did not help and has bad thoughts that this has happened." Soon other people will blame this family too, and then they will say about the family: "It is because they are witches and they do not want to help other people that there is so much sickness or famine." And then the family finds out about it because people "act strange." But nothing is done to the family; "they are just talked about." No one wants bad things said about him or his family, and this family will then try to help the village in work and with the ceremonies. If this family does not do this, then people will continue to think that they are witches and the family will have a hard time because "people will talk about them and act strangely toward them."

There are apparently no open accusations of witchcraft, no trials, and no executions. In this respect the Hano and the Hopi too differ radically from the Zuni and the Indians of the Rio Grande pueblos. Witchcraft lore is enormously rich among Indians in all the pueblos except Hopi. I suspect that witchcraft gained in elaboration from Spanish contacts; as for witch hunts, trials, and executions, these seem to be definitely of Spanish derivation. Witchcraft trials and executions fit into a Spanish or European pattern among Indians of the Rio Grande pueblos and at Zuni, where they have occurred until fairly recently (see Scholes 1935: 218 ff.).

At every major Hano ceremony the Village Chief admonishes the people to live properly. He may, at times of unusually bad behavior or in times of severe drought, send a special Kachina character to both kivas to plead for proper conduct and to urge everyone to keep a "good heart." Thus, for example, in February 1951 a Kachina impersonator representing a bear visited both kivas and warned the people against excessive drinking.

The Chief of the Outside Kiva clans tells his people to observe the admonitions of the Village Chief and lectures his group on proper behavior during the Winter Solstice ceremony. The War Chief (see Hano ceremonial officers, Chapter 5) in the past had the duty of maintaining order and discipline in the village. Formerly, it is reported, he had the authority to whip miscreants and often exercised this right, but today the War Chief is restricted to announcing cooperative enterprises and to taking a prominent part in social dances.

The Kachina collectively arouse fears of the supernatural and the unknown and are for children particularly, a strong force for exacting conformance to Tewa mores. Until recently, Hano had a group of masked bogeymen called *Saveyoh* different from the Hopi *Soyoku*. The War Chief designated persons to represent *Saveyoh* and visit the village at certain specified times during the year. While they were about, all children were supposed to remain indoors, for these ogres were especially "fond" of children. Parents whose children needed disciplining would threaten to feed them to the monsters and would often permit their children to get a glimpse of the frightening creatures as they walked past the house.

Hano has now adopted the Hopi bogeymen, or Soyoku, and these impersonators appear with those of the First Mesa Hopi. Thus, about midmorning of the final day of the Hopi Powamu ceremony in February, the Soyoku impersonators start to visit all the homes where there are children. The group spends about five to ten minutes in front of each house, peering inside and often going partly into the house. In homes in which there is a child whose behavior has been reported to them as being very bad, they pretend to try to carry off the frightened child. While this struggle is going on, other members of the group bargain with the family for a food ransom. When a satisfactory ransom has been obtained, the Soyoku move on to another home where they repeat the performance.

The Soyoku make only one appearance a year, but parents constantly remind their children of them in order to compel obedience. The annual visits of the ogres are exceedingly traumatic experiences for the child. An acculturated Tewa gave me the following account of his childhood recollections and reactions to the Soyoku:

When I was a little boy I wished that our house would be the first one to be visited by the Soyoku. But that never happened, for we lived almost at the other end of the village. As I heard the Soyoku coming nearer and nearer the perspiration would start running all over me. Some children cried, but I just tightened up and felt like I was going to die. My aunts (*kiyu*, father's sisters) always came to tell me that the Soyoku would not carry me away, but my mother would say that I was very bad and that she didn't care if the Soyoku took me. When the Soyoku arrived, my aunts would fight with them to keep them away from me. My mother would bring corn meal and meat to give to the Soyoku, and she would say to me: "See how bad you've been, I have to give them all the food we have so they won't take you." That would make me feel very bad, for I felt that I was responsible for my mother giving all the food away. I would then run to my mother and grasp her dress crying: "Don't let them take me; I will be a good boy; I will work hard and get back all the food you've given to the Soyoku." Even after I was initiated and knew that the Soyoku were just ordinary people I would get frightened when I heard the noises they made.

There is an increasing disapproval of the visits of the bogeymen, particularly among wage-earning families. Another acculturated Tewa, a government employee, declared that he would not permit his children to witness the activities of the Soyoku because he felt that "they were too frightening" and that his children did not need such disciplining.

Hopi Tribal Council and Tribal Court

The Hopi Tribal Council came into being as the result of the Indian Reorganization Act of 1934 which permitted and encouraged the establishment of tribal governments. In 1936 the Hopi Indians adopted a tribal constitution and bylaws, formed with the aid of government specialists. The constitution

(U.S. Department of the Interior 1937) authorized the establishment of a council and a court. Nine political units or voting districts were established, the division being based chiefly on the native feeling of unity among the villages. The four communities on First Mesa—Walpi, Sichomovi, Hano, and Polacca—decided to work together, and thus First Mesa is considered one unit. Because the other villages were unable to reach an agreement in terms of larger groupings, each is considered a separate unit. Second Mesa forms three units: Mishongnovi, Shipolovi, and Shongopovi; Third Mesa, four units: Oraibi, New Oraibi, Hotevilla, and Bakabi; and the irrigation-farming community of Moenkopi is considered another unit.

Representation in the first Tribal Council was distributed as follows: First Mesa 4, Mishongnovi 2, Shipolovi 1, Shongopovi 2, Oraibi 1, New Oraibi 2, Hotevilla 2, Bakabi 1, and Moenkopi 2. The officers consisted of a chairman, vice-chairman, secretary, treasurer, sergeant-at-arms, and interpreters. The duties of the Council include the regulation of tribal funds and tribal commercial enterprises; the maintenance of law and order on the reservation; the protection of tribal arts, crafts and ceremonies; and giving of advice to the government with regard to appropriations for the benefit of the tribe.

The council has met only sporadically since its organization and in most respects is considered a failure. Traditionally, tribal unity is foreign to the Hopi Indians. Apparently they are not ready to become organized as a tribe at the present time (see Titiev 1944: 67–68; Eggan 1950: 108–109). The council has received support primarily from the people of First Mesa. The Hano Tewa enthusiastically supported the work of government specialists who were helping to draft the Hopi constitution and were largely instrumental in "selling" the idea to the Hopi (La Farge in manuscript). The Tewa's friendly and cooperative attitude toward the government and toward whites in general and their traditional role as go-betweens have helped to unite the villages of First Mesa and to convince them of the benefits that tribal unity will bring. The assumption of secular roles is traditionally correct, for the Hano Tewa and the First Mesa Hopi in recent years have generally let the Tewa lead in matters dealing with the external affairs of the group.

The Hopi Tribal Court follows a law-and-order code established by the Secretary of the Interior (U.S. Department of the Interior 1940: 243–246). It operates independently of the Indian Service under a judge, assistant judge, and two policemen. The Hopi Tribal Court hears both Hopi and Navaho cases. Most of the cases are concerned with assaults, trespass, disorderly conduct, and driving while intoxicated. In the winter of 1950–1951 I learned of only two Tewa who appeared before the Tribal Court; they were charged with driving while intoxicated.

Summary

Analysis of Hano social organization reveals lineal kinship ties as paramount over community or village bonds. In the section that follows ceremonial organization too will be seen to depend heavily on lineal kinship relations. Historically the Tewa undoubtedly once had a stronger village organization and compared with Hopi villages, community integration at Hano is considerably stronger at present. In the kinship system there is a retention of Tewa terms, and traces of the bilateral, generational emphasis are evident in kinship behavior. Moiety rationalizations persist in the grouping of clans and in migration legends. Social control, as with the Hopi, is restricted mainly to the household and lineage, but important controls are exercised on the village level. In recent years through intermarriages with First Mesa Hopi, Hano social institutions and behavioral patterns have become adjusted to Hopi ones, but Hano has given as much as it has borrowed. The exchange has brought about a remarkably high degree of social integration on First Mesa. A tribal organization might have succeeded for the villages of First Mesa, but the strong clan system of the Hopi mitigated against an organization based on nonkinship principles for the entire Hopi tribe.

5

Religion and Ritual

HANO RELIGIOUS ORGANIZATION and ceremonies are not as complex as the Hopi, but bear similarities to those of the latter. Yet, despite these resemblances, affinity to the New Mexico Tewa is also evident in virtually all areas of Hano religion and ritual. Basic in the organizational pattern of the religion are the two-kiva pattern and the clans associated with the kivas. The core of the ceremonial system is the Kachina cult and the ceremonial association system. Kachina performers are drawn from members of clans which belong to the kivas and the performances are fitted into the Kachina cycle of Walpi. The Kachina cycle begins with the Hopi Powamu ceremony in early or mid-February and ends with the Hopi Niman ceremony in July. No Kachina dances are given in the intervening period, but other ceremonial association events occur at this time and "social dances" may be performed during the non-Kachina season.

Ceremonial associations, as among the Hopi, are "owned" and managed by a clan. Some association ceremonies occur at fixed times during the year; others may take place at a time specified by the leaders of the clan which own and manage the association.

Kachina and ceremonial association performances have both public and private (or secret) aspects. The private portion of a ceremony involves the periodic prayer retreat of the association, the erection of an altar prior to a public ceremony in the clan house, and the costuming of the dancers and participants. The public feature of the ceremony is held either in the village courtyard or in the kiva and is open to both Indian and white visitors.

The "social dances" of the Hano are secular performances. They occur among the Hopi as well as among the New Mexico Pueblos. At Hano they may be initiated by any man or woman who will assume the responsibility of selecting the dances, arranging song and dance rehearsals, and setting the time for its public presentation. Social dances consist of small group dances and at Hano they typically consist of buffalo, deer, butterfly, and war dances. Excepting the butterfly dance, these dances reveal numerous innovations and have "Plains" or pan-Indian characteristics.

The foregoing has been an outline of Hano religious organization and ceremonies. It is important now to examine Hano religion and ritual more closely in order to understand its basic features and underlying concepts. In the analysis that follows I will attempt to present the important details of Hano religious organization and also try to indicate the changes and adaptations the Tewa of Arizona have had to make in a new social and physical environment. It is clear from even a casual study of Hano religion and ritual and an examination of the historical accounts of Hano that until recently the most pronounced difference between the Hano Tewa and their Hopi neighbors was in ceremonial organization. Both groups were reluctant to borrow or give up ceremonies and ritual activities. Although the kinship and clan systems were adapted comparatively early to approximate Hopi systems, the Hano Tewa steadfastly clung to their own unique ceremonial organization. In the past fifty or sixty years, however, there has been a pronounced breakdown of Hano ceremonial organization and a greater adaptation of the organization to that of the Hopi. The breakdown is due partly to the extinction of the Sun clan, but probably the most important factor is the growing acceptance by the Hopi of the Tewa as equals.

Kiva Organization

Hano has two kivas: Court Kiva and Outside Kiva. Clan affiliation determines kiva membership. Members of the Bear, Corn, Tobacco, and Fir clans belong to Court Kiva; members of the Earth, Cottonwood, and Cloud clans belong to Outside Kiva.

As we have previously noted, Fir clan was formerly aligned with the Outside Kiva group of clans. At the time of the extinction of the Sun clan, or when its extinction was imminent, the Fir and Bear clans apparently seized upon a casual mention of the two clans as partners in a migration legend as an excuse to merge. The merging bolstered the membership of the Bear clan, which at the time had almost died out. For the Fir clan, this linkage placed it in the prestige group of clans. The merging of the two also substituted the Fir for the Sun clan and made possible the performance of ceremonies in the Court Kiva in which four clans participated.

Formerly, the chieftainship of the village, which is also that of the chief of Court Kiva, went in turn to each of the four clans of the kiva. The last two Village Chiefs, however, have been Bear clan members; apparently their appointment was an attempt to conform to the Hopi pattern of selecting the Village Chief from that clan. Reports regarding the number of years a Village Chief is supposed to serve before relinquishing his office in favor of another clan are conflicting. Some informants reported that his term is four years, others that it is for life. All are agreed that a chief can be removed if he proves unsatisfactory; that is, if illness or drought conditions persist during his tenure. The clan chiefs would meet and arrange the removal of such a chief by simply agreeing among themselves to recognize the clan chief who would ordinarily succeed the incumbent once the latter had served his term. No other action would be taken, but public sentiment would be so strong against the chief that he would abdicate.

The Village Chief functions as the ceremonial head for all of Hano. The welfare of the Tewa of Hano is his basic concern. He is supposed to watch over his people and to succor and protect them by means of prayers for rain and for physical well-being, and he is directly responsible for the proper performance of all ceremonies. The duties of Village Chief are considered sacred, and he as a person is not supposed to take an active part in disputes or quarrels.

The Winter Solstice ceremony, the most important of the Tewa ceremonies, is under the direction of the Village Chief. This is an annual gathering of all men of the clans belonging to that kiva. Formerly an altar was erected, and considerable ritual was associated with the ceremony (Stephen 1936: 39–41; 49–51), but today the ceremony is comparatively simple. An altar is no longer erected. It is reported that the last Winter Solstice Chief requested that all the Winter Solstice paraphernalia be buried with him. Informants relate that he was disturbed by the loss of knowledge of the proper performance of the ceremony and wanted the function discontinued after his death. Since learning the legends recited in the ceremony is extremely difficult, their disappearance is easy to understand.

The Winter Solstice ceremony has been briefly described in connection with the life cycle in the preceding section. A few remarks will be added here. On the final night of the ceremony, stories and clan legends are related. These tales recount the Hopi petition for Tewa aid and tell of the hardships the Tewa encountered after their arrival at Hopi. No Hopi are admitted to this ceremony, for the stories are definitely intended to malign their hosts. Many of the legends are sung as ballads. Those recited in Court Kiva differ in certain respects from those related in the Outside Kiva. The latter kiva has a number of war ballads which are their own unique possessions as a warrior group. The most characteristic feature of the dance that accompanies these songs is that the men form a circle while they sing and slowly dance around a single drummer. The formation and tempo of the songs are similar to those of the Plains Indian "circle" or "round dance" songs. At regular intervals the singers emit war whoops. The songs contain refrains that tell of Tewa bravery against the Utes, Navahos, Paiutes, and other neighboring nomadic Indian tribes, or recounts Tewa war magic, prowess, and the like.

Before the extinction of the Sun clan, a member of that clan functioned as Sun Watcher for all of Tewa Village. He was an assistant to the Village Chief in all important ceremonies, but also had his own duties. He was responsible for setting the time of all ceremonies in the annual Tewa cycle and for announcing the ceremonial dates to the village. His position was in certain respects analogous to that of the War Chief in the Outside Kiva. Both functioned as assistants and made announcements; the Sun Watcher announced items of a ceremonial nature, and the War Chief made known secular functions or instructions pertaining to war. The Hano Tewa now look to Walpi for the announcement of all important ceremonial dates.

The group of clans belonging to the Outside Kiva, although recognizing the ceremonial preeminence of the Court Kiva clans and accepting the Bear clan head as Village Chief, functions in many respects as a separate and distinct unit. The existence of this dual division at Hano has prompted an early student of the Hopi and Tewa (Parsons 1936: xliv–xlv), to speak of the situation as a survival of the New Mexico Tewa dual division or moiety system. The Hano kiva groupings are in fact similar to the moiety divisions of the New Mexico Tewa pueblos. Each group has a chief who functions separately and is said to be independent of the other. The Hano Tewa, like the New Mexico Tewa, also conduct two separate initiation rites, one for each group or moiety. The Hano Tewa organization, however, differs in that one group of clans—the Court Kiva group—is more important than the others, and the chief of the Court Kiva clans is the head of the whole village. At present, ceremonial and secular responsibilities are no longer transferred seasonally from one group to another as among the New Mexico Tewa. Parsons (1936: xlv), however, reports that seasonal transfer ceremonies were still being conducted in 1920.

It is important to remember that the Hano are a remnant group of the Southern Tewa; the Tewa still in New Mexico are the northern branch of the tribe (see Chapter 1). Thus, the differences that we note today between the two groups of Tewa may have already existed in the past rather than changed through contact with the Hopi.

Formerly, the Outside Kiva group consisted of the following clans: Fir, Earth, Cottonwood, and Cloud. The merging of the Fir clan and its alignment with the Central Plaza Kiva, however, leaves only three clans in the Outside Kiva. The chief of this group of clans for the last fifty years has been an Earth clansman, but his predecessor was a Cottonwood clansman (Parsons 1936: xliv). The chief of this group of clans rotated in the same manner as the position of the Village Chief among the clans of the Court Kiva group.

The functions of the Outside Kiva clans are ideally concerned with war and secular affairs. In general, these clans, with respect to the Court Kiva clans, occupy a position analogous to that of the whole of Hano with respect to Walpi. Thus the Outside Kiva clans are charged with the physical protection of the Court Kiva group. Members of the latter group are supposed to pray and go into retreat for a successful victory, but the Outside Kiva group is supposed to meet the enemy and engage it in battle. The assignment of "duties" to clans mentioned in the preceding section is a familiar Hopi custom. This concept may have been borrowed by the Hano Tewa; the duties are not assigned to individual clans, however, but to the two kiva groups.

The chief of the Outside Kiva group has an assistant called simply the War Chief, who is the head of the Cottonwood clan. Whether this position, like that of the Village Chief and the Outside Chief, also went in succession to a clansman of each of the member clans could not be conclusively validated; the reports of informants regarding the rotation of this office were conflicting and uncertain. The man who at present is the War Chief has been in so long that it seems unlikely that the position ever alternated among the four clans. The Outside Kiva Chief and the War Chief were responsible for the successful operation of a war and directed battle activities. The War Chief was charged with leading and directing periodic tribal hunts, and announced all cooperative enterprises such as the cleaning of springs, spinning parties, working parties, and the like, for the Village Chief. Maintenance of order and discipline in the village were also responsibilities of the War Chief.

The main responsibility of the Outside Kiva Chief, as with the Village Chief, is the Winter Solstice ceremony. This ceremony differs little from the ceremony in Court Kiva and is held at the same time. The Outside Kiva clans sing "war ballads"; the singing of these is considered their special prerogative. The Earth clan head, who today is the chief of the Outside Kiva group of clans, still erects his altar for this ceremony. Because the former Court Kiva Chief was buried with the Winter Solstice ceremony paraphernalia, as noted previously, the present Court Kiva Chief conducts a simple ceremony without an altar.

Kiva membership in either kiva is determined by a person's clan affiliation, but for men it is confirmed at the time of the Winter Solstice ceremony. At this ceremony, boys fourteen to eighteen years of age are formally inducted into the appropriate kiva.

Ownership of Tewa kivas, like that of the Hopi kivas, is ascribed to the clans that took the initiative in building them. The use of the kivas, however, is restricted to the clans believed to belong together. The Corn clan owns Court Kiva and the Earth clan owns the Outside Kiva. In any function for which the kiva is used, a member of the clan—usually a brother or uncle of the head clanswoman—that owns the particular kiva acts as caretaker. This man is also often referrred to as Kiva Chief but his job is to take care of the structure; his position is not a ceremonial office. This man receives the gifts of food that are brought by women to ceremonial participants. During the night Kachina dances he obtains an ear of corn from every troop of dancers and sprinkles sacred corn meal on all the participants. While a dance is in progress he periodically shouts approval and encouragement and may often request a performance to be repeated.

Associations and Ceremonies

THE KACHINA CULT   At once the most arresting and the most characteristic of Pueblo ceremonies are the Kachina rites. Everywhere among the Pueblos the Kachina cult is concerned with supernatural beings somewhat vaguely connected with ancestral spirits. These supernaturals are believed to have the power of bringing rain and general well-being to Pueblo communities if properly petitioned through ceremonies made as beautiful as possible and given joyously without ill feelings toward anyone or toward any aspect of the universe. There are many types of Kachina, some of animals and birds such as owl, eagle, bear, mountain sheep; others are identified by some characteristic aspect of their appearance: the Long-Beard Kachina, the Left-Handed Kachina, and so on; still others are called by the sounds they emit. There are more than

200 Kachina types among the Hopi and Tewa, but some dozen or so appear to be the most popular and are the most frequently represented in the dances. Only men impersonate the Kachina in the ceremonies; women are not permitted to don Kachina masks and costumes. Kachina dancers may be all of one kind, paired, or of mixed types. The number of dancers usually varies with the number of men in a particular kiva, the usual number being between twenty and thirty.

Kachinas are also represented as dolls made from cottonwood root. These wooden figurines are carved and painted in the likeness of the masked and costumed impersonations. At the ceremonies these dolls are given to little girls and are generally conceived to be symbolic of life—human, animal, and plant.

Until recently, the Kachina cult of Hano was quite different from that of the Hopi. Tewa Kachinas reputedly came from a mythological lake northeast of Hopi—that is, from the "original land of the Tewa." In contrast, the "home" of the Hopi Kachinas is in the San Francisco Peaks near Flagstaff, Arizona, west of the Hopi villages. Two members of the *Koyalah*, a ceremonial clown association, participated and "brought" the Kachina impersonators to each of the Hano kivas for a one-night ceremony. There were four such Kachina night ceremonies, spaced equally throughout the year. The first ceremony occurred sometime in December or January, the second in March or April, the third in July or August, and the fourth in October or November. Apparently the Hano Kachina ceremonies have been extinct so long that the names of the ceremonies and information regarding the clans or kiva groups responsible for their performance are hopelessly confused. The December or January Kachina ceremony was called *Kavenah,* and the July or August ceremony, *Suyukukwadih.* Parsons gives *Tiyogeo* as the name for the March ceremony and equates it with the Rio Grande seasonal transfer ceremony (Parsons 1936: xliv). My informants did not recognize the name given by Parsons, nor that it had reference to a "transfer"; they did, however, remember a Kachina ceremony celebrated in March or April. Parsons also reports an October seasonal transfer ceremony but does not give a name for it (Parsons 1936: xliv). This ceremony is apparently the fourth Kachina ceremony reported by my informants. I was unable to learn the names for the second and fourth Kachina ceremonies.

The original Hano Kachina cult and ceremonies are obsolete; Hano Kachina dances now follow the pattern of First Mesa as a whole and fit into the seasonal cycle directed by the Powamu association of Walpi. The Powamu association requires each of the Hano kivas to select a group of Kachina impersonators who perform first in their own kiva and then visit in turn all the other eight kivas on First Mesa (two at Hano, two at Sichomovi, five at Walpi). The present Kachina initiation rites, although performed by the Hano Court Kiva, are identical with those of the Hopi at Walpi, as far as my informants knew. All reported that both the present cult and initiations are recent; they did not know what took place in the earlier cult initiations, although they believed that they were quite different. Initiation into the Kachina cult, as presently practiced, has been described in Chapter 4 under Life Cycle.

THE CLOWN ASSOCIATION   The *Koyalah,* or clown association, of the Hano Tewa was apparently very much like the Rio Grande Tewa clown organization, the *Kosa.* Its part in the Kachina ceremony has been mentioned. In addition, the *Koyalah* appeared in several main dances, particularly courtyard dances in which large numbers participate, such as the basket or corn-grinding dances. During such a dance the clowns carried on side exhibitions for the amusement of spectators. By previous arrangement they often sought out individuals and carried them to the center of the plaza to ridicule them in view of all the spectators. The association is now extinct. Clown impersonators today, although still referred to as *Koyalah,* are appointed only for a particular occasion and do not comprise an association.

THE CURING ASSOCIATION   The *Sumakolih* is a curing association whose members wear masks like Kachina impersonators. The *Sumakolih,* now controlled by the Cloud clan, was formerly owned and managed by the extinct Sun clan. The association cures "sore eyes"; but any Tewa or even a Hopi from First Mesa may request the association to dance, either to effect a personal cure or to secure well being for the community in general. A ceremony is held in August or September, in which the association inducts new members. Members are drawn from both Hopi and Hano. Since the Cloud clan is virtually extinct, I was told that the association will probably die out with the death of the old Cloud clansman who is at present head of the association (see The Clan, Chapter 4).

In addition to the established association for curing, there are individual Hano shamans, or doctors. These have a good practice, not only at Hano but among the Hopi of all the mesas and the Navaho as well. Hano shamans are respected and renowned for their successful healing practices. Undoubtedly they have this reputation because of their Rio Grande Pueblo ancestry. Among these Indians curing receives a major emphasis in their ceremonial ritual.

RECRUITMENT OF ASSOCIATION MEMBERS   Members for Hano ceremonial associations are recruited in the same manner as for the Rio Grande Tewa associations: by vow of parents before the birth of a child, by vow of either a severely ill person or his parents, or by trespass into an area enclosed by a line of meal where the particular association has erected its altar for its annual or major ceremony. In addition, entrance may be purely voluntary, as among the Hopi. In each case a ceremonial sponsor is selected in the manner described in the preceding section.

OTHER CEREMONIAL ACTIVITIES   The Winter Solstice ceremony has already been discussed. Actually there are two such ceremonies, one in each kiva, conducted independently of the other, although they take place on the same day and coincide as well with the final night of the *Soyala,* or Winter Solstice ceremony of the Hopi at Walpi. Before the position of Sun Watcher lapsed, it is reported, the Tewa chose their own time to hold the solstice ceremonies, and this was not necessarily the same as the final night of the Hopi *Soyala.*

At any time during the year the chief of the Court Kiva or the chief of the Outside Kiva may gather the men of his kiva to engage in prayer-stick making, but this does not occur at any specified time in the annual cycle. Prayer sticks are made and deposited in order to bring rain or to insure good health. Such activities start in early morning and are usually finished by mid-afternoon, when the prayer sticks are taken by one or two men to be deposited in the various Hano shrines and in the springs that belong to the Tewa village.

Initiation

The initiation of Hano children into the Kachina cult is almost identical with that of the Hopi. All Hano Tewa are eventually initiated into the cult (see Life Cycle in Chapter 4). Only Court Kiva is empowered to conduct Kachina initiations; members of clans of the Outside Kiva must come to Court Kiva to be initiated.

Initiation, or induction, into the kiva group is uniquely Hano; the Hopi do not have kiva initiation. The initiation is only for men and is the closest approach the Hano Tewa have to the elaborate Hopi tribal initiation (see Titiev 1944: Chapter X). Hano kiva initiations suggest the moiety initiations of the New Mexico Tewa, but differ from them in certain essential features. Thus, the New Mexico Tewa moiety initiations are elaborate affairs and induct both men and women (Hill, in manuscript), whereas the Hano Tewa rites are simple rituals and are restricted to men. All Bear, Fir, Tobacco, and Corn clansmen between fourteen and eighteen years of age are inducted into Court Kiva; young men of corresponding ages belonging to the Earth, Cottonwood, and Cloud clans are inducted into the Outside Kiva. In early times the initiation may have been more complex (see Parsons 1926: 212), but today the initiates merely attend the final night of the Winter Solstice ceremony with their ceremonial fathers. The inductees receive a new name from their ceremonial fathers and may thereafter attend all important functions of their kiva.

Kachina and kiva initiations of the Hano Tewa appear to be reversed when compared with similar New Mexico Tewa ceremonies. Kachina initiations among the New Mexico Tewa are restricted to boys and occur sometime after the boy is fourteen years of age; moiety initiations, however, which confirm membership into one of two groups, induct children of both sexes of an age comparable to those of Hano children inducted into the Kachina cult.

The present Village Chief, from whom I obtained the major part of the information presented in this chapter, made the following statement about the present status of ceremonial life at Hano:

When the Sun clan people were still with us, Hano was like a separate pueblo. We were not bound by the ceremonial dictates of the Walpi leaders. Our Sun clan determined the position of the sun and the phases of the moon. Without recourse to Walpi we started our own prayer-stick making in the kivas and celebrated our private and public ceremonies separately from Walpi. It is true that in those days there was bad feeling between Hopi and Tewa, but we were strong then and we did not mind what the Hopi thought about us. Now I have to wait until the Walpi chief has announced Soyala [the Hopi Winter Solstice ceremony] before I can go into the kiva at the Hano Tewa Winter Solstice ceremony. This is true of all other ceremonies that we have—before we start them we must consult with Walpi. When I was a youth my grandmother and my granduncles used to tell me that the Hopi did not like us to hold separate ceremonies; they accused the Tewa of "playing around with their wives" while they were in retreat. When the Sun clan became extinct and the office of Sun Watcher disappeared with it, we had to give into the Hopi. Since that time we have been slowly losing our ceremonies, and my position as Hano village chief is no longer as important as it was in my grandparents' generation. My hands are bound; I can act in ceremonial matters only with the approval of the Walpi chief. We may all become Hopi some day, but I keep telling the young men at the Hano Tewa Winter Solstice ceremony what is my responsibility as Village Chief. That is, to impress upon all of us that we are Tewa and different from the Hopi and that we must always remember this. The young people do not take these things seriously, but it is my duty to tell them.

The dates of the major Hopi and Hano Tewa ceremonies are determined eight or sixteen days before the event occurs. The Hano chief is notified by Walpi leaders when he can start his ceremonies. Hence, in ceremonial affairs he is completely subordinated to Walpi religious authorities. It would seem, therefore, that with the disappearance of Hano ceremonial life, secular positions will become increasingly important. Indeed, the respect and prestige enjoyed by the Hano Tewa interpreter, a purely secular position, seems to justify such a prediction. Hopi ceremonial organizations have already made considerable headway into Hano society and will probably eventually displace the earlier system. First Mesa appears to be moving toward an integration that will be characterized by a rich Hopi ceremonialism and a high degree of political cohesion achieved through the secular interests of the Hano Tewa.

Social Dances

A diversity of dances not part of the Kachina cult and ceremonial associations are called "social dances" by both the Hopi and the Hano Tewa. These dances are open to the public, white and Indian, and are primarily secular. In fact, however, all Pueblo ceremonies have religious overtones, but some are more religious and esoteric than others. The rites of the Kachina cult and ceremonial associations, for example, are the most sacred, while the "social dances" are the most profane. Yet no Pueblo ceremony is completely serious and austere either; even the Kachina and association rites have humorous and entertainment aspects.

Social dances are of many types, but animal and war dances probably prevail. Some of these dances are obviously very old, going back to early Tewa-Plains contacts. Social dances are performed, as we have noted, primarily for entertainment; they also differ from the more esoteric rites in that novel forms are permitted and improvisations are constantly being introduced. Thus, traditonal Pueblo costumes have been modified with the addition of mirrors, sleigh bells, and colored feathers. The songs and dance steps retain basic Indian patterns, however, and Euro-American features are absent.

For arranging all the social dances for one year, excluding those in the regular ceremonial cycle, two men are chosen from each kiva group to act as supervisors. Their duties consist of collecting all the needed paraphernalia, choosing a drummer, selecting the girls who are to dance, and assisting the dancers to put on their costumes and make-up before each appearance. In addition, they see that the kiva is in proper order and that sufficient wood is brought to keep the place warm for rehearsals and for the final day of the dance.

A dance of the New Mexico Tewa called *panchale*, "prisoner's dance," has become increasingly popular on First Mesa in recent years. *Panchale* has apparently no religious significance. It has some resemblance to white American social dancing, but the New Mexico Tewa claim that it is old and native with them. Boys choose girls (sometimes there are "lady's choice" dances as well!), and about ten or more couples dance to the beat of a drum and a chorus of singers. A song and dance has several sets similar to the Virginia reel. One complete dance with its series of variations lasts for about fifteen minutes. The tempo is lively and a round of dancing leaves the young dancers breathless and flushed.

I was told that the Hopi objected to the dance when it was introduced, about twenty years ago, on the ground that it was "not Indian!" Panchale is extremely popular on First Mesa today, however, although it is not danced during the Kachina season and, so far as I know, it is danced nowhere else on the Hopi reservation but at Hano. Young Hopi and Hano boys and girls are enthusiastic about Panchale and come from other villages to join in.

Beliefs and Values

The Hano Tewa hold a world view generally characteristic of all the Pueblos. This is the premise that man and the universe are in a kind of balance and that all things are interrelated. There is no dichotomy between good and bad; evil is simply a disturbance in the equilibrium which exists between man and the universe. The activity world of man, of the natural environment of plants and animals; the inanimate world of earth, rocks, and dead vegetable matter; the ethereal world of wind, clouds, rain, and snow; even the "thought world" of human beings are all believed to be in a state of balance. The activity world is one of cooperative helpfulness; everyone works for the good of the whole. Individual subordination to group effort is believed to be an essential part of maintaining balance in the universe. Logically the "thought world" is a happy one, free of ill feeling or hostile attitudes toward any aspect of the universe. Illness, prolonged drought conditions, famines, and all other misfortunes are believed to occur as the result of a disturbance in the orderly nature of the universe.

Unfortunate happenings come, in the Pueblo Indian's belief, not as a punishment or retaliation by a supreme being or beings, but because of a break in the interrelatedness of the universe. Man alone can disturb the orderliness and harmonious balance of the universe. He may break it by ill feeling toward another, or toward a number of individuals; indeed, even by disliking or perceiving ugliness in some aspect of the universe. He may do so by taking more food than is necessary for sustenance, or by not being generous in sharing and giving what he has, He may break the balance by killing more game than is essential to supply himself and his relatives with food or by taking more clay or more pigment than is necessary to make needed pottery vessels.

Not only must man use sparingly of the food and material resources of the universe but he is required to reciprocate by appropriate propitiatory rites. These range all the way from offering corn meal, corn pollen, prayer feathers, and prayer sticks to elaborate ceremonial dances made "as beautiful as possible" and participated in by the whole village.

The importance of ceremonies as propitiatory rites to effect well-being and bring much needed moisture to parched lands is well known to students of Pueblo culture (cf. Haeberlin 1916). The associated and essential requisites of cooperative effort and a happy state of mind, however, have generally been ignored. It is significant, therefore, that as early as 1912 an anthropologist made the following insightful observation: "The assertion is made [by the Pueblos]: 'It will rain; we are happy; it will rain; we are dancing; we are dancing; it will rain.' Cause and effect are hardly differentiated. Let us hope all people are happy, but let us make sure that they are dancing." (Aitken 1930: 382)

The Pueblo individual examines his thoughts and attitudes to make sure that he is in a "happy state of mind," but he is also concerned with the actions and thoughts of his fellow man. If he is satisfied with his actions and his state of mind and still misfortunes and illness persist, then he is ready to cast blame on someone else. Hence, the constant surveillance of the behavior of one's neighbors, even of close relatives. Since an individual's misbehavior brings misfortune not only to himself but to the group as a whole, all members of one society are suspect until the guilty one is discovered. During disease epidemics, crop failures, and drought conditions Pueblo villages are fear-ridden communities. Pueblo authorities watch closely the behavior of village members to determine the culprit or "witch." Gossip and accusations of witchcraft run rampant in the village as a whole. The lot of the individual who cannot account for curious or deviant behavior is extremely grave. If his behavior remains peculiar and misfortunes persist, he falls prey to the community. Traditional sanctions of ridicule and witchcraft accusations make his life miserable. In extreme cases he may be banished from the village (see Chapter 4, Social Control).

There is no evidence that Hano itself was ever an anxiety-ridden community or that it was ever rent with internal strife. The Tewa of Hano appear to have taken over the more positive aspects of the Pueblo world view, while their more outgoing personality characteristics and their marginal position with respect to the total Hopi society have prevented the development of intravillage suspicions and conflicts. The Hopi as convenient scapegoats also helped to drain off the hostilities that might have been turned destructively toward their fellow Tewans.

Ritual Activities

Since the Hano Tewa have permitted many of their own ritual activities to lapse, they now cooperate in various ways to keep First Mesa Hopi ceremonies operating efficiently within the annual ceremonial calendar. However, only in terms of the Kachina cult, which is organized, like that of the Hopi, in kiva groups, do the Tewa actually participate in Hopi ceremonial life. As participants in the Kachina cult, the Tewa are wholly under the direction and supervision of the Powamu association. Although the Tewa are permitted to choose the Kachina characters they impersonate, they must synchronize their performances to correspond with those of all the other kiva groups on First Mesa. There are nine kivas on First Mesa, including those of Tewa Village, and each has a Kachina group. Each kiva group presents its own dance without consulting any of the other groups; indeed, it is part of the show to keep the audience in suspense until the moment the troupe comes down the kiva ladder. Spectators go into any one of the nine First Mesa kivas—usually the one nearest to home—to see all nine performances, since each kiva group starts in its own kiva and then visits all the other eight kivas successively. In February and March, Kachina performances are held inside the kiva and occur weekly on Saturday nights. Saturday night Kachina dances are a recent adjustment made necessary by off-reservation employment and boarding schools. From April until the end of the Kachina season (in July), the dances are less frequent and are usually given outdoors in the village courtyard.

The Niman, a Hopi ceremony, occurs in mid- or late July and marks the return of the Kachina to their home in the San Francisco Mountains, according to Hopi belief. During the rest of the year until the following Powamu, no masked or Kachina dances are permitted by the Hopi. In the past the Tewa frequently violated this mandate and provoked much ill feeling. There are still occasional infractions by the Tewa, such as the appearance of the Shumakoli Kachina in August or September and an occasional "social dance" in the Kachina season, when such dances are prohibited. But such violations are becoming less frequent with the loss of strictly Tewa ceremonies and the increasing desire of the Tewa to cooperate with the Hopi and to appear favorably in their eyes.

The end of the First Mesa Kachina season terminates the direct participation of the Tewa in ceremonial activities. During the rest of the year the Tewa assist the Hopi with their ceremonies and act as hosts along with their neighbors for all visitors to First Mesa. Tewa women work industriously in the preparation of food for their Hopi husbands and for other Hopi relatives who are actively engaged in these ceremonies. The men perform various services for their Hopi kinsmen. All share in the festive occasions and open their houses to all visitors.

During that part of the year when Kachina dances are forbidden and the Kachina are reportedly away in the San Francisco Peaks, the Tewa give frequent social dances in which only a small group of unmarried men and women usually participate. Many of the dances have been borrowed from other tribes, usually from the Rio Grande Tewa, and in these the war theme is frequently introduced. As the dancers emerge from the kiva, Plains war-dance songs are sung, and the War Chief dons his best war costume and periodically emits an ear-splitting war whoop. The men also try to appear like their Rio Grande Tewa kinsmen by braiding their hair or by wearing false braids. Today, many New Mexico Tewa journey to Hopi in order to teach the Hano Tewa new songs and dances and to appear with them in the dances. The Hano Tewa in turn make frequent visits to the Rio Grande Pueblo area.

Summary

Before 1900 the Tewa and Hopi were pronouncedly distinct in ceremonial organization. The present kiva organization, association, and ceremonial ritual, despite surface similarities, indicate differences that were undoubtedly sharper at an earlier period. Initiation into the Kachina cult now, however, is almost identical with that of the Hopi. Apparently with the disappearance of their own Kachina cult, the Tewa have adopted the Kachina practices of the Hopi. Adaptation to the Hopi Kachina cycle seems to have completely replaced the earlier cult and the ceremonial cycle consonant with it. Kiva initiations, however, remain uniquely Hano. They resemble the Rio Grande Tewa moiety initiations on the one hand, and the Hopi tribal initiations on the other. The elaborate ritual practices of both New Mexico Tewa and Hopi, however, contrast sharply with the simple, one-night ceremony of the Hano Tewa.

The Hano world view is typically Pueblo, but the suspicions and intra-village bickering so characteristic of Hopi and other Pueblo Indians are virtually absent at Hano. As a minority group and with the Hopi as scapegoats Tewa hostilities have been largely directed outside the village.

The adjustment of religious institutions and concepts to Hopi counterparts appears to be the most important characteristic of the Tewa at present. Hano participates wholeheartedly in the first Mesa Kachina cycle. At other times of the year they engage enthusiastically in social dances. Although they rarely join Hopi associations, they cooperate with the Hopi in all their ceremonial activities and, with their neighbors, act as hosts to all visitors.

6

Livelihood

THE MOST CHARACTERISTIC ASPECT of Hano and Hopi economics is the exchange system—the method by which food, services, and certain types of goods are exchanged. These practices link all of the peoples on First Mesa and at times involve Hopi from more distant villages as well. The system operates within the household, clan, linked clans, kiva groups, and between the three communities on First Mesa. Exchanges occur on specific occasions in an individual's life cycle (puberty, entrance into a ceremonial association, and at marriage), and are an integral part of every ceremonial rite. These practices have prevented economic stratification; the Hopi and Tewa population is essentially on an equal economic footing. In addition to this economic leveling effect, these activities have contributed to the increasing trend toward social and cultural integration on First Mesa. This section will attempt to reveal the nature of these exchange practices and to expose the characteristics of the economic system generally.

Economic Pursuits

The Tewa of Hano, like their Hopi neighbors, are still basically horticulturists. Livestock and wage work, however, have become increasingly important in recent years. These economic activities are potential threats to the integrity of the clan structure and may eventually result in social reorganization. At present, however, the Tewa, as well as the Hopi of First Mesa generally, are handling the new economic pursuits largely in terms of traditional experience. Sharing of work and food has helped to prevent the segmentation of the society into nuclear family units. Although a family that has wage workers or sheep and cattle may live as a nuclear family for long periods, it reverts to extended-family living and assumes clan responsibilities once it is back at Hano. These fluctuations between nuclear-family and extended-household living and the participation in clan responsibilities and privileges occur with great frequency. With families owning sheep and cattle, these fluctuations are usually seasonal: nuclear-family living in the summer, extended-household living in the winter. The families who are engaged in wage work in Keams Canyon revert to extended-household living on week-ends. The rich Hopi and Tewa social and ceremonial cycle also brings back nuclear-family units to participate as extended-household units and to resume clan duties and responsibilities.

Land

Land is the most important possession of the Tewa and Hopi. The Tewa report that in exchange for the services they rendered as "warriors" and "protectors" of the Hopi on First Mesa they were given lands extending northward from this mesa. According to the Tewa, one of the primary inducements for coming to Hopi was the offer of assertedly productive land. Old men relate that their forefathers were deceived by the Hopi. The land was poor and no amount of hard work could make it produce the crops they were promised. Their storehouses were often empty, and they suffered through the drought-stricken years. But the Tewa, like the Hopi, learned to overcome the rigors of the environment.

The Hopi country poses many difficult problems for farming. Only by ingenious and ardous methods of planting and caring for their growing crops have the Hopi and Tewa garnered a living from the land (cf. Stewart 1940). The rainfall is scant, averaging only about ten inches per year. The altitude of 6000 to 6500 feet brings early and late frosts that limit the growing season to barely three months. In July and August sudden cloudbursts are common and cause considerable damage. To insure a crop against these odds, a Tewa or Hopi farmer plants two or three fields, which he chooses with great care. Kirk Bryan's observation of Hopi-planted fields is applicable to Tewa farming practices:

> The areas utilized are variable in size and location, but each is chosen so that the local rainfall may be reinforced by the overflow of water derived from higher ground. The selection of a field involves an intimate knowledge of local conditions. The field must be flooded, but the sheet of water must not attain such velocity as to wash out the crop nor carry such a load of detritus as to bury the growing plants. Such conditions require a nice balance of forces that occur only under special conditions. Shrewd observation and good judgment are necessary in the selection of fields. (Byron 1929: 445)

Ownership and Inheritance

There have been some changes recently in ownership and inheritance. These changes are due to modern conditions; cash income from livestock sales and wage work have increased individual property. Formerly a man had only a few possessions he could call his own; now he often has money and buys numerous articles. Property acquired by a man in this way is usually inherited by his sons or is specifically transmitted to certain persons before his death. Despite these changes, however, the basic pattern of earlier times still continues with respect to the ownership and inheritance of land and houses.

Land originally assigned to the Tewa has been divided into clan plots which are set off by stone symbols marked to represent the various clans and placed along sight lines. Within a clan plot, the mother of each family has several fields at her disposal. When her daughters marry, a woman gives each of them one or more plots of land, or parts of several. Upon her death, female matrilineal relatives assume control of the land, the direct descendants having prior claim. The question of disposal of lands to married daughters has often little practical importance, since the daughters continue to live in the house and with the family of the mother.

Men have no right to ownership or inheritance of land; they work it, however. When a man marries, he relinquishes his right to work on his own clan lands and works his wife's. Before he marries, a young man works on his own clan lands, and he may return to them in the event of a separation or divorce. The farm hands in a typical Hano extended household include a woman's father, her unmarried maternal uncles, her bachelor brothers, her husband, her unmarried sons, and the husbands of her sisters. This is, of course, not true in households where wage work and/or livestock activities are of major importance; in these the number of men engaged in horticultural activities is much smaller.

Houses and household equipment, like land, are owned and inherited in the female line within the household and lineage. A woman may give certain sections of her house for the use of one of her daughters when she marries, or, with the help of men of her family—her husband, brothers, sons—she may erect a new house for the couple, or an addition to the old one; or she may simply receive her son-in-law into her own house. All the furnishings and equipment within a house also belong to the senior woman of the household; a man owns only the clothes and jewelry that are on his person.

In contrast to the land and the houses, horses, cattle, and sheep are generally the property of men. When a man marries or divorces, he takes his own personal flock or herd with him. The care of sheep and care of cattle are male occupations. Although a woman may often inherit or acquire shares in flocks, her husband or one of her male relatives is given the task of caring for them.

Wage Work, Livestock, and Horticulture

Before wage work, livestock, and horticultural activities are discussed, it is important to realize the cooperative nature of the communities on First Mesa. Marriage and kinship ties and the economic responsibilities involved in these relationships interrelate all of the three villages. The conventional economic analysis, liberally supplied with statistical tables indicating per capita or family incomes, may have meaning in our society but blur the true economic picture of a highly cooperative society such as that of the Hopi and Tewa.

Most of the Tewa wage income derives from employment at the Hopi Agency in Keams Canyon, twelve miles from First Mesa. During the period of intensive fieldwork (1950–51) the total cash income from government employment for Hano was $58,500. Livestock sales netted another $22,100. In addition, there were other sources of cash income such as nongovernment employment, compensations to servicemen's dependents, Social Security benefits, relief obtained from the Indian Service, and arts and crafts (particularly pottery) amounting to an additional $20,000. The total annual income amounted roughly to $100,000 in 1950–1951. The table below summarizes the economic activities of persons nineteen years of age and above, and thus indicates those individuals bringing in cash income and those contributing to subsistence. The population of Hano at this time was 405 individuals including those resident on the reservation as well as the few living off the reservation (the present population is about 500; compare Dozier 1954: 287).

The cash income figures distort the true economic situation on First Mesa by de-emphasizing the role of horticulture and the importance of the economic exchange practices. As cash income horticulture is negligible, but Tewa and Hopi crops still furnish the basic subsistence for the people. In addition to its economic importance, the central position of horticulture among these three villages is revealed by the cutoms and activities of the people. Ritually, these pueblos revolve around horticulture. All ceremonies have as their main theme the propitiation of the spirits so that they will make the crops bountiful. It is not only in religion, however, but also in secular activities that horticulture is stressed. From spring to fall the Tewa and Hopi are in the fields working to produce crops from an inhospitable environment. Harvest time is a period of feasting and gaiety. Everyone is happy and all generously exchange and share in the fruits of the land.

The table shows that more than one-half of the employable persons are still engaged in horticulture or in handicrafts (115 out of 203). The 88 livestock owners and wage workers are also, of course, periodically occupied with farming, and all share in the farm produce. It is important to point out that there is a great deal of overlap in economic activity; that is, almost all men work for wages periodically and/or have sheep and cattle. All women make pottery and do housework; in addition, many of them work occasionally for the government. The table thus lists only *primary* economic activities. However, when involvement in traditional economic activities is considered, it is evident that horticulture is still basic to the Tewa.

Cooperative Enterprises

Income figures, it must be repeated, do not give us the complete economic situation at Hano or on First Mesa. It is essential to describe the intricate exchange and cooperative activities of these people in order to understand Tewa and Hopi economics.

The household functions constantly as an economic unit; its members as-

PRIMARY ECONOMIC ACTIVITIES OF EMPLOYABLE PERSONS
(Ages nineteen years and above, except the very old)

	Primary Economic Activity	Men	Women	Totals
Cash Operation	Livestock owners	43	0	43
	Government employment	25	2	27
	Employed off reservation	10	8	18
	Totals	78	10	88
	Farming at Parker*	7	6	13
	Horticulture on reservation	50	0	50
	Handicraft (pottery, tanning, weaving)	25	27	52
	Totals	82	33	115
	Total engaged			203

* Parker, Arizona—an area of irrigated farmlands on the Colorado River recently made available to Hopi, Navaho and other Southwestern Indians.

Source: Data compiled during fieldwork; see Dozier 1954:359.

sist one another in daily duties and see that all are properly fed and clothed. Food sharing and the exchange of services in larger units of the society operate in relation to the social and ceremonial functions which occur with remarkable frequency and regularity. A quick review of such functions that occurred in 1950 is worthwhile here. In the month of January there were seven weddings and two social dances; from February to May there were weekly Kachina dances. June and July were busy months in the field; but there was one social dance and a water-spring cleaning operation in June, and in mid-July the Tewa joined the Hopi with their Niman festivities. August was an occasion for another social dance, two more weddings, and the Hopi Snake Dance. In September and October the Tewa were busy with harvest; but a Shumakoli ceremony was celebrated in mid-September, and in late October the complex tribal initiation ceremonies began at Walpi.

Social and ceremonial functions have a leveling effect and prevent the segmentation of the population into rich and poor. Money as such is not contributed or divided; it is food—including tobacco and cigarettes—that is distributed. This food is either home grown (that is, farm produce and livestock products) or it is bought in trading posts or off-reservation towns for the purpose of distribution. Tewa culture prescribes that everyone should give generously, and the givers expend much effort to donate large amounts. Since production and income derived from wage work, livestock, handicrafts, and other sources vary among the households, the amount of food given is not the same from each household. Division of the food among the receivers, however, is equal and this has a leveling effect. The kind of social or ceremonial function determines who is to give and who is to receive. In certain functions—a wedding, for example—those benefiting from food gifts are essentially restricted to the bridegroom's clan and linked clans, whereas the givers are mainly members of the bride's clan and linked clans. At a wedding, however, the bride's garments are woven and furnished by the groom's relatives. In a kiva group ceremony, such as a social dance or a Kachina dance, the members of the group of clans that belong to the particular kiva sponsoring the ceremony are both givers and receivers. Such a function operates in the following manner. Women belonging to these clans carry the food to the kiva, and the men of the clans receive it. The food is divided equally by the kiva chief and his assistants among all the men participating in the ceremony. When the food has been divided, it is taken by the men to their respective households. A man will thus take back some of the food contributed by members of his own household, but he will also have some of the food contributed by all the other households. Hence, a variety of food products is taken back. As a rule, those households contributing more will receive less, and those giving little will receive more.

Ceremonial functions in larger units operate in much the same manner as has been outlined above for the kiva groups. Food in cooperative operations of this sort is also contributed by women and is divided equally in the kiva or kivas by the men and taken back to their respective households when the ceremonies are over.

In connection with these cooperative enterprises, work has to be done. The givers buy groceries, butcher cattle and sheep, prepare food, and carry it to the kivas. The receivers are also constantly working either in prayer or in the many tasks required to make the particular ceremony successful. All such work is done cooperatively, with gaiety and good fellowship.

The sharing of food and exchange of services, as noted previously, operates through specific social and ceremonial customs in a hierarchy of units: household, clan, kiva group, community, and the whole of First Mesa. Illustrations of the kind of activity involved in each one of these cooperative enterprises is described in the following pages. The household, though not dependent on social and ceremonial functions, is described first because it is the crucial economic unit.

HOUSEHOLD SHARING AND EXCHANGE   I have selected one more or less typical unit to illustrate food sharing and the exchange of services within the household. This household belongs to the Corn clan and consists of an old Tewa couple, their two daughters who are married to Hopi men, and their children. The relationship is shown in the following figure; the names used are fictitious.

This extended family lives separately in three family units for indefinite periods: Paul and Edith, the old couple, live by themselves in an old house at Hano; Marie, their younger daughter, and her husband, Peter, and their children live in a separate house, also at Hano; and the older daughter, Jane, who works at the Hopi Indian Agency, lives with her husband, John, and their children in government quarters at Keams Canyon. In the summertime Paul and Edith move to their ranch house, where Paul tends his sheep and cattle, assisted

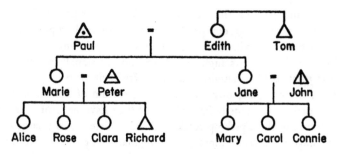

○ △ Tewa Corn clan

△ A different Tewa clan

△ A Hopi clan

△ A second Hopi clan

A Tewa Household.

Tom is married to a Walpi woman and belongs to a different household; he has no economic relations in his sister's household. He frequently visits his sister, however, and she consults with him in important ritual matters and refers to him all difficult cases of disciplining her children and grandchildren.

by Edith's brother, Tom, and often by other male members of the Corn clan. Two or more of the grandchildren are usually with the old couple on the ranch.

In the summertime the nuclear family of the two daughters is thus reduced, with some of their children living on the ranch of the old couple. The younger daughter remains on the mesa top with her young children; the older daughter continues with her regular job at Keams Canyon, assisted in household chores by her older daughter, while her younger daughters spend the summer at the ranch.

During the summer months John and Peter, Jane's and Marie's husbands, respectively, farm a portion of the Corn clan lands belonging to their mother-in-law, Edith. Paul, when not busy with his cattle and sheep, gives his sons-in-law a hand with their farming activities, and in return they often help him with his livestock. John and Peter are also occasionally employed by the government and thus contribute a sporadic cash income. Both Hopi husbands also help their own Hopi clan relatives who own cattle and sheep.

In the winter the situation changes somewhat. Although Keams Canyon is twelve miles from First Mesa, Jane comes with her husband and children every week-end to spend Saturday and Sunday with her parents. Since Marie and Peter and their children live at Hano, they are constantly visiting with the old couple and exchanging services with them. In winter, as in the summer, the Hopi men are periodically on the government payroll. John works irregularly as a stonemason, and Peter occasionally works for the Indian Agency as a day laborer. John and Peter have no cattle and sheep, but some of their clansfolk have some, and John and Peter often assist them in herding activities.

Marie and Jane on their frequent visits to their parents bring food, either from their stores of garden produce or from the trading posts. Both daughters work cooperatively with their mother—cooking, grinding corn, and the like. The old couple frequently slaughter a sheep and occasionally a calf or cow, and portion the meat to their daughters on their frequent visits.

Paul, the old man, owns a wagon and a team of horses. The team and wagon are used by the sons-in-law whenever they have need of them. Recently Jane and John bought a pick-up truck, and the vehicle has to a large extent displaced the wagon and team. Since Jane is regularly employed at Keams Canyon, she made the initial down-payment on the truck, I was told, and John and Peter helped her on the monthly payments. Paul drives a car, and until he became blind about a year ago, he used the truck as much as John. At the present time the old couple ask one of their sons-in-law to drive for them whenever they wish to go anywhere. Peter uses the truck for transporting his immediate family or for performing services for the benefit of the extended household. I was told that the person using the car at a given time is supposed to pay for gas and oil and for light repairs; for major repairs a contribution is taken from all adult members of the household. Hopi and Tewa give their cars rough treatment. The farms and ranches to which they travel most frequently are situated in remote areas, and roads are extremely bad. During the initial phases of my study when I lived in one of the Tewa households, my 1949 jeep station wagon became household property, and since none of the members could drive, I was the chauffeur. I hauled sheep, calves, and wood in my car and transported members of the household to various parts of the reservation, and on several occasions to the off-reservation towns of Gallup, Holbrook, and Winslow.

The major portion of daily interaction, sharing, and cooperation goes on within the household unit. In social and ceremonial functions embracing larger units, activity is initiated within the household but is intricately fitted into the larger cooperating units, whether clan, kiva group, community, or intervillage.

CLAN AND LINKED CLAN SHARING AND EXCHANGE   The clan and its linked clans (see Chapter 5) function as economic cooperative units in many social and ceremonial functions. For an illustration of the activities in such an interacting unit, a wedding has been selected. A wedding is primarily a social event, but like all other activities of the Hopi and Tewa, it also has ceremonial features.

The Wedding to be discussed is one between a Tewa Cottonwood girl and a Hopi Butterfly boy which took place in January 1950. The boy had been secretly courting the girl, and presumably had been having sexual relations with her. (The boys sneak out together, and each meets his sweetheart at a secret rendezvous or at her house after her family is asleep.) Sanction of the marriage was obtained when the girl took up residence with the boy's family at Sichomovi and was permitted to stay. Immediately she began to grind corn in a darkened corn-grinding room. Theoretically she was supposed to grind corn for three days and four nights by herself, but actually all her clanswomen assisted. Not only did the women of her own Cottonwood clan help, but also those of the Hopi Kachina clan, which the Hopi consider related to that clan. These women ground corn in their own homes and brought it to her and also assisted her in the darkened room, in which she remained the traditional four-day and four-night period.

In the meantime the boy's male relatives on both his father's and his mother's side prepared the girl's wedding garments; these consisted of a belt, robe, dress, and moccasins. These items of clothing are the only contributions made by the boy's relatives; all of the other gifts are contributed by the girl's relatives.

While the girl was grinding corn, the men of the girl's clan and linked clans brought food to the bridegroom's house; during this four-day period they slaughtered sheep and cattle, brought firewood, and helped the women carry the food. A special room, about 15 by 20 feet, was set aside to hold the food gifts. At the end of the four days the room was entirely filled with food—basins of stew, roasted meats, stewed peaches, yellow corn-meal cakes, sugar-frosted baked cakes, pies, and other foods covered the entire floor space; sacks of wheat flour were piled almost to the ceiling against one wall; on the opposite side, piki was stacked like cordwood halfway up to the ceiling. On the last day, when most of the food was brought in, five pick-up trucks drove into the plaza in front of the bridegroom's house and unloaded enormous trays of corn meal. Each truck contained about a dozen trays, approximately fifteen to twenty inches in diameter, heaped with tightly compacted corn meal to a height of two feet or more. Large flour-sack cloths were tied about the trays to protect the corn meal. Some trays were so heavy that it required three or more men to lift and carry them.

The food brought by the girl's family was shared by the clansfolk of the bridegroom and also by those of the linked Badger clan. On the evening of the fourth day all the women of these clans visited the boy's house and were given large quantities of food to take home with them, each woman receiving an approximately equal amount.

KIVA GROUP SHARING AND EXCHANGE   In certain social and ceremonial functions the unit of cooperative activity is the kiva group, that is, the clans belonging to one of the two Hano kivas. These functions occur with less frequency than clan-phratry functions but are similar cooperative affairs, differing only in that more people take part in them. The activities that characterize kiva group enterprises will be illustrated by a discussion of a social dance.

On June 24, 1950, a *Yandewa* dance was given by members of Court Kiva at Hano. For a whole month previously, however, preparations and rehearsals had been under way. The Yandewa is a colorful dance originally borrowed from Santa Clara Pueblo. There are four dancers in each of eight courtyard appearances—two young men and two girls—thirty-two dancers in all. All the men belonging to the clans of the kiva join in the chorus and help in many other ways inside the kiva. For this occasion I made a trip to Santa Clara Pueblo (a Tewa village in New Mexico) and brought back with me three men from this village. As honored guests we were permitted to watch all the preparations for the dance inside the kiva.

Twice during the day of the dance, first at midday and again in late afternoon, all the adult women of the clans that belong to Court Kiva—Bear, Corn, Tobacco, Fir—brought in enormous quantities of food. On each occasion the kiva chief distributed the food equally among all those present in the kiva. My share was two washtubs of bread, crackers, candy, piki bread, and various other foods. In addition, there were large quantities of prepared foods in bowls and pans such as stews, roasted meats, jerky (sun-dried strips of beef), corn-meal gruel, and the like. The prepared foods were also divided as equally as possible among the men. After each "giving," the men carried their portions of the food to their respective homes. I presented my share to my hosts at Hano.

COMMUNITY SHARING AND EXCHANGE   Cooperative enterprises that are essentially communal include hunting, planting, harvesting, cleaning springs, and gathering firewood for the kivas. Such enterprises are initiated by one of the men; they are announced by the War Chief and are participated in by all able-bodied men, while the women grind corn and cook to feed the whole community. After such an enterprise, the men gather in the kiva to offer thanksgiving or to put on a social dance, and the food is given and shared, as described above, for the Yandewa. Each man, with his share of food, then returns to his own household.

The following account of the general requirements and procedure of a working party (cf. Parsons 1925: 112–115) was related to me by one of my Tewa informants:

Whenever a man decides to have a working party he asks permission from the Village Chief. The petition is made by presenting the chief with a basket or bowl of corn meal. If the chief accepts the meal the petitioner starts preparations right away. He makes several prayer feathers and abstains from meat and salt for four days. During this time he must not sleep with his wife. At the end of four days he asks the War Chief to announce the working party to the whole village. The petitioner then supervises the work, but he is assisted by all of his clanspeople and his paternal aunts [i.e., women of his father's clan]. All those men who are not actively engaged in the work are put to other tasks. Some of the men must go for firewood, others for water and cattle. Women and girls must grind corn and prepare food to feed not only the men actively engaged in the working party but the entire village. Everyone helps to make the working party a success. While working all the people are happy; jokes and stories are told so that work becomes like play. Later there is a dance given by the kiva groups, and everyone goes home loaded with food.

INTERVILLAGE SHARING AND EXCHANGE   First Mesa Hopi ceremonies of major importance, such as the tribal initiation which occurs in certain years in November, the Powamu ceremony in February, the Niman in July, and the Snake Dance in August, are occasions in which all three villages cooperate. Only a few Tewa are active participants in Hopi ceremonies, but marriage ties with the Hopi relate them to participants in these ceremonies. Tewa women are thus as active as Hopi women in preparing and buying food to be taken to the men who are participating in the ceremonies. Tewa men are busy butchering, hauling wood, and making food supplies available for the women. Teams and wagons, and more recently, automobiles are put to use to assist in the transportation of foodstuffs. The contributed food is taken to the Walpi kivas in which these ceremonies take place; division and disposal of the food operates in the manner described for kiva group ceremonials above. The day of the dance is given over to elaborate feasting, every home setting out food for guests from other Hopi villages and for Indian visitors from other tribes. In recent years special white friends have also been honored as guests. The festive spirit and cooperative activity of the people of First Mesa in a major ceremonial is an impressive sight.

TRADING PARTIES   Another cooperative activity of First Mesa villages is the trading party. This activity is initiated by a household and is open to anyone in the three villages; indeed, visitors, Indian or white, may participate. My wife was a frequent "trader" during our residence at Polacca. Trading parties occur with great frequency, "about two or three times a month," my hostess reported.

Most of the participants are women, though men are not barred. Men are supposed to contribute game, and when I appeared for the first time at a trading party, the women greeted me in a chorus: "Where is your deer meat; where are your rabbits?" But they took the cigarettes, soft drinks, and wheat flour I brought, and I received in return hot tamales, piki, and doughnuts.

The trading party is held outdoors, in front of the house of the family that initiates it. The food, clothing, and other articles brought by those participating are spread out on the ground, while the "traders" stand around in a circle. The articles brought to be traded are extremely varied. I have seen chinaware, shoes, overalls, and toys (bought in town), along with the more common items such as Hopi pottery and baskets, piki, oven-baked bread, meat stews, cakes, pies, and wheat and corn flour.

There is very little bargaining at a trading party. Hopi and Tewa trade in a friendly, noncompetitive fashion. A "trader" walks to the article that catches his fancy, finds out who the owner is, and then trading is conducted between the two people. The food or goods traded are generally those displayed; but if a person who wishes an article does not have an item at hand which the owner wants in exchange, she may mention a number of articles at home which she is willing to give for the desired article. Exchanges are made in the most agreeable and friendly manner. I saw no attempts "to drive a hard bargain." The people seem to have no notion of getting more for an item, or one of a better quality, in exchange. When I asked my hostess why the trading parties were so popular, she replied:

> Because we have a good time; we joke, laugh, and tease each other when we trade. In the evening we return home with a variety of things. Some people don't have meat, others have no flour, or piki, or cigarettes; we trade and everybody gets the things they want.

Summary

It is evident that while horticulture is still basic in Hano economy, wage work and livestock have come to form a very important part of their economic system. At present the social organization of Hano is still operating chiefly in terms of the traditional patterns of the extended-household and clan structures. A number of factors have brought about this situation. First, livestock and wage-work activities, particularly the latter, are recent innovations. Secondly, modern transportation facilities have made possible frequent resumptions of extended-household living and interaction in terms of clans and linked clans. Thirdly, the satisfaction derived from the extended household and clan and the rich ceremonial life of community living have not been matched elsewhere.

The exchange system operating in a hierarchy of social units has prevented pronounced differences in the economic standing of Tewa families and generally of the families in all three communities on First Mesa. These practices are remarkably strong and complex and indicate continuity into the future, despite modern pressures. The cooperation of Tewa and Hopi in these functions points to greater cohesion in the future, thus minimizing social barriers between the two groups and working toward a coalescence of First Mesa society.

7

Perspective and Outlook

IGRANTS to the Hopi country, the Tewa established their village within calling distance of the nearest Hopi community. For a long time they persisted in maintaining cultural and linguistic distinction from their neighbors. Recently these barriers appear to have been lifted and a trend toward assimilation established. In this study the present community has been described in the context of Hopi society and culture and with reference to the social and cultural patterns of their ancestors, the New Mexico Tewa. The accommodating devices for and against assimilation have been explored and possible reasons for this situation have been suggested. In these final pages, I will only speculate briefly about the destiny of this Tewa community.

It is difficult to isolate aspects of Hano society and culture that may be unique to the group since affinities to both New Mexico Tewa and Hopi appear in all areas. There is one aspect, however, in which the Tewa seem to differ from both Hopi and New Mexico Tewa; this is in the realm of personality. The Hano Tewa appear to be more aggressive, and more willing to accept white ways and to cooperate with the local Indian Service. The individual Hano Tewa is friendly to whites and has little of the reticence characteristic of both the Hopi and New Mexico Tewa.

What factors are responsible for creating a personality structure at variance with that of other pueblo peoples is not clear. Certain hypotheses may be ventured, however. First, the Hano Tewa were formerly on the eastern frontier of the pueblo area, and there they interacted with Plains Indian tribes. Second, they had a history of resistance to the Spaniards but escaped to Hopi before becoming completely subdued. Third, their minority status at Hopi may well have demanded the assertion of personality traits antithetical to the Hopi. At Hopi, the aggressive, independent traits of the Tewa were encouraged by their position as warriors and protectors of the Hopi.

Any one or all of these factors may account for the formation of Hano

Tewa personality. The fact is that, at present, Hano attitudes and behavior contrast sharply with the Hopi.

In spite of Hano's friendly and cooperative relations with whites, the people have not lost their cultural identity as they have adjusted to the impact of American ways. Hano culture appears to be well integrated along traditional lines. Certain important changes have come about, however, as the result of modern pressures. The most important are the periodic reductions of the matrilineal extended household to meet demands imposed by livestock and wage-work activities. As a result of modern conditions, too, a few of the young people, particularly those who have gone to schools outside the reservation, are encountering problems of adjustment. The older people make much of this, yet these deviations from the norm may express no more than the behavior characteristic of the younger generation in any society.

Although it is possible to see both Hopi and New Mexico Tewa elements in Hano social and ceremonial organization, these have been so thoroughly integrated into Hano culture that the group differs significantly from the other two. As might be expected from the long residence of the Tewa on First Mesa, their culture more closely resembles that of the Hopi. Thus, Hano social and ceremonial organization is founded on the same principles as the Hopi: the kinship system, household, clan, ceremonial societies, and kiva groups. But in all these institutions certain similarities to the New Mexico Tewa appear—areas in which they differ from the Hopi.

The greatest difference between Hano and Hopi culture is in ceremonial organization. The dual or moiety concept is emphasized among the Tewa, not only in migration legends and myths, but in actual structural make-up. The two kiva groups at Hano function independently of each other in the performance of various ceremonials. There is a leader, or chief, for each group, as among the New Mexico Tewa. The Hano Tewa hold kiva group initiations that are suggestive of Tewa moiety initiations in New Mexico. Until recently Hano had a Kachina cult, essentially different from that of the Hopi but closely resembling the New Mexico Tewa Kachina organization. In the emphasis on curing in their ceremonies, the Hano Tewa again contrast with the Hopi and indicate retention of New Mexico Pueblo concepts.

Hano social and ceremonial organizations thus appears to be the result of (1) a core of elements indigenous to the group and bearing resemblances to the New Mexico Tewa, (2) elements borrowed from the Hopi over a period of two and a half centuries during which the two groups have lived as neighbors, and (3) a unique integration of the two that appears to be becoming progressively a new whole.

Hano economy is still to a large extent dependent on farming, handicrafts, and other traditional occupations, although wage work and livestock raising have become much more important in recent years. The economy is still functioning mainly in terms of the traditional patterns of the extended-household and clan structures. A number of factors have helped to make these patterns viable. First, livestock and wage-work activities, particularly the latter, are recent innovations. Second, modern transportation facilities have made possible frequent resumptions of extended-household living and interaction in terms of clans and groups of clans. Third, the satisfactions derived from the extended household, clan, and the rich ceremonial life of community living have not been matched elsewhere.

Potential threats to the household and clan structures are, however, clear. The Tewa's increasing relations with whites are drawing them more and more into the American pecuniary economic system. It is possible that as succeeding generations grow up, away from the close touch of the extended household and clan relatives, the importance of the nuclear family will increase. New generations may find satisfactions with a new pattern of relationships and value systems. On the other hand, native customs are strong and complex and apparently will long continue despite modern pressures. The Hopi and Tewa have thus far adjusted to modern conditions, and there is no reason why they cannot continue to make such adjustments while preserving most of their own traditional social and ceremonial organization.

Orthographic Note

Transcriptions of native terms are only phonetic approximations in so far as this is possible with the use of English sound symbols. Tewa speech sounds differ radically from English and other European languages. The glottal stop, tone, vowel length, glottalized consonants, and nasalized vowels all occur as contrastive features. Unfortunately it has not been possible to indicate these characteristics of Tewa phonology in this case study. For a more exact phonetic transcription of the native terms used in this study the reader is referred to the following publications of the author:

1. "The Hopi-Tewa of Arizona," *University of California Publications in American Archaeology and Ethnology*, Vol. 44, No. 3, 1954.

2. "Kinship and Linguistic Change among the Arizona Tewa," *International Journal of American Linguistics*, Vol. 21, No. 3, July 1955.

References

ADAMS, ELEANOR B., AND FRAY ANGELICO CHAVEZ, eds., 1956, *The Missions of New Mexico, 1776.* Albuquerque, N.M.: University of New Mexico Press.

AITKEN, BARBARA, 1930, "Temperament in Native American Indian Religion," *Journal of the Royal Anthropological Institute,* No. 60.

ASCH, S. E., in manuscript, *Personality Development of Hopi Children.* Reported in Thompson, Laura, 1950, *Culture in Crisis, A Study of the Hopi Indians.* New York: Harper & Row, pp. 94–95.

BEADLE, J. H., 1878, *Western Wilds, and the Men Who Redeem Them; An Authentic Narrative.* Cincinnati.

BLOOM, L. B., 1931, "A Campaign Against the Moqui Pueblos," *New Mexico Historical Review,* Vol. 6, No. 2, pp. 158–226.

———, 1936, "Bourke on the Southwest," *New Mexico Historical Review,* Vol. 11, pp. 217–282.

BOLTON, H. E., 1916, "The Espejo Expedition, 1582–1583." In H. E. Bolton, *Spanish Explorations in the Southwest, 1542–1706.* New York: Charles Scribner's Sons, pp. 161–196.

BRYAN, K., 1929, "Flood-Water Farming," *Geographical Review,* Vol. 19, No. 3, pp. 444–456.

CALHOUN, JAMES S., 1915, *The Official Correspondence of James S. Calhoun.* Washington, D.C.: Bureau of Indian Affairs, Government Printing Office.

CRANE, LEO, 1925, *Indians of the Painted Desert.* Boston: Little, Brown & Company.

DOZIER, EDWARD P., 1954, "The Hopi-Tewa of Arizona," *University of California Publications in American Archaeology and Ethnology,* Vol. 44, No. 3.

———, 1955, "Kinship and Linguistic Change Among the Arizona Tewa," *International Journal of American Linguistics,* Vol. 21, pp. 242–257.

EGGAN, FRED, 1950, *Social Organization of the Western Pueblos.* Chicago: University of Chicago Press.

HACKETT, C. W., and C. C. SHELBY, 1942, *Revolt of the Pueblo Indians of New Mexico and Otermin's Attempted Reconquest, 1680–1682.* Coronado Historical Series, Vols. 8 and 9, Albuquerque, N.M.: University of New Mexico Press.

HARRINGTON, J. P., 1912, "Tewa Relationship Terms," *American Anthropologist,* n. s., Vol. 14, No. 3, pp 472–498.

HILL, W. W., in manuscript. "Santa Clara Pueblo." In the possession of its author, Department of Anthropology, University of New Mexico, Albuquerque, N.M.

HODGE, F. W., G. P. HAMMOND, and AGAPITO REY, 1945, *Revised Memorial of Alonzo de Beuavides, 1634.* Coronado Historical Series, Vol. IV. Albuquerque, N.M.: University of New Mexico Press.

LA FARGE, OLIVER, 1936, in manuscript. Personal notes on the organization of the Hopi tribe, 1936.

NARVAEZ VALVERDE, FRAY JOSÉ, 1937, "Notes upon Moqui and Other Recent Ones upon New Mexico." In C. W. Hackett, ed., *Historical Documents Relating to New Mexico, Vizcarja, and Approaches Thereto, to 1773,* Vol. 3. Washington, D.C.: Carnegie Institute of Washington, pp. 385–387.

PARSONS, E. C., 1921, "Hopi Mothers and Children," *Man,* Vol. 21, No. 58, pp. 98–104.

———, 1925, *A Pueblo Indian Journal, 1902–21,* Memoirs of the American Anthropological Association, No. 32. Menasha, Wis.

———, 1926, "The Ceremonial Calendar of the Tewa of Arizona," *American Anthropologist,* n. s., Vol. 28, No. 1, pp. 209–229.

———, 1936, "Introduction." In E. C. Parson's, ed., *Hopi Journal.* Columbia University, Contributions to Anthropology, Vol. 23, Part 1, pp. xxv–lii.

SCHOLES, F. V., 1935, "The First Decade of the Inquisition in New Mexico," *New Mexico Historical Review,* Vol. 10, No. 3, pp. 195–241.

———, 1942, *Troublous Times in New Mexico, 1659–1670.* Albuquerque, N.M.: Historical Society of New Mexico, Publications in History, Vol. 11.

STEPHEN, A. M., 1936, *Hopi Journal,* edited by E. C. Parsons. Columbia University, Contributions to Anthropology, Vol 23, Parts 1 and 2.

STEWART, G. R., 1940, "Conservation in Pueblo Agriculture," *Scientific Monthly,* Vol. 51, No. 4.

THOMAS, A. B., 1932, *Forgotten Frontiers, A Study of the Spanish Indian Policy of Don Juan Bautista de Anza, Governor of New Mexico, 1777–1787.* Norman, Okla.: University of Oklahoma Press.

TITIEV, MISCHA, 1944, *Old Oraibi, A Study of the Hopi Indians of Third Mesa.* Cambridge, Mass.: Papers of Peabody Museum of American Archaeology and Ethnology, Vol. 22, No. 1.

THOMPSON, LAURA, 1950, *Culture in Crisis, A Study of the Hopi Indians.* New York: Harper & Row.

THOMPSON, LAURA, and ALICE JOSEPH, 1944, *The Hopi Way.* Lawrence, Kans.: United States Indian Service.

U.S. DEPARTMENT OF THE INTERIOR, 1894, "Moqui Pueblos of Arizona and Pueblos of New Mexico." In *Report on Indians Taxed and Indians Not Taxed in the United States at the Eleventh Census, 1890.* Washington, D.C.

———, 1937, *Constitution and By-Laws of the Hopi Tribe, Arizona.* Washington, D.C.: U.S. Office of Indian Affairs.

———, 1940, *Code of Federal Regulations, Title 25—Indians,* Chapter 1. Washington, D.C.: U.S. Office of Indian Affairs.

Recommended Reading

COLTON, HAROLD S., 1949, *Hopi Kachina Dolls*. Albuquerque, N.M.: University of New Mexico Press.

An excellent discussion of the Hopi Kachina cult, impersonations of Kachina characters, and the manufacture of Kachina dolls. Superb photographs and illustrations of many Hopi Kachina types.

DENNIS, W., 1940, *The Hopi Child*. New York: Appleton-Century-Crofts.

An observational study of child care and child rearing techniques among the Hopi.

DOZIER, EDWARD P., 1961, Rio Grande Pueblos. In Edward H. Spicer, ed., *Perspective in American Indian Culture Change*. Chicago: University of Chicago Press, pp. 94–186.

A historical survey of Rio Grande Pueblo society and culture and a comparative analysis of religious and social organization.

EGGAN, FRED, 1950, *Social Organization of the Western Pueblos*. Chicago: University of Chicago Press.

An excellent study of the Pueblo communities of Hopi, Hano, Zuni, Acoma, and Laguna. In addition, Eggan has provided a comparative survey of the Rio Grande Pueblos.

LANGE, CHARLES, 1958, *Cochiti: A New Mexico Pueblo Past and Present*. Austin, Tex.: University of Texas Press.

An exemplary study of a modern Keresan Pueblo community in the context of its past and present.

O'KANE, WALTER COLLINS, 1950, *Sun in the Sky*. Norman, Okla.: University of Oklahoma Press.

A popular and sympathetic account of Hopi life, industries, and interests. Excellent photographs of people and the mesa-top-communities.

PARSONS, E. C., 1939, *Pueblo Indian Religion*. Chicago: University of Chicago Press.

An encyclopedic two-volume work covering all aspects of Pueblo Indian religion, social organization, and the changes brought about by contacts with other peoples.

THOMPSON, LAURA, and ALICE JOSEPH, 1944, *The Hopi Way*. Chicago: University of Chicago Press.

A summary of the results of psychological tests on Hopi children made by a research team of social scientists. Good information on Hopi socialization techniques and an excellent summary of Hopi social and ceremonial organization.

THOMPSON, LAURA, 1950, *Culture in Crisis: A Study of the Hopi Indians.* New York: Harper & Row.

Presents the integrative aspects of Hopi culture and emphasizes the problems Hopi Indians face in adjusting to white culture.

TITIEV, MISCHA, 1944, *Old Oraibi: A Study of the Hopi Indians of Third Mesa.* Cambridge, Mass.: Papers of the Peabody Museum of American Archaeology and Ethnology, Vol. 22, pp. 1–277.

A study of the social and ceremonial organization of the Hopi Indians of Third Mesa and a superb analysis of the distintegration of "Old Oraibi" over factional disputes.

WHITMAN, WILLIAM, 1947, *The Pueblo of San Ildefonso.* New York: Columbia University Press.

Presents an outline of New Mexico Tewa Pueblo social and ceremonial organization and the adjustment problems of these Indians to increasing white contacts.

CPSIA information can be obtained
at www.ICGtesting.com
Printed in the USA
FFHW011711240719
53839530-59532FF